BLACK POLITICS AND RACE:

A Contemporary Reader on Racism and Black Politics

Edited by
Henry A. Bryant, Jr.

University Press of America™

Copyright © 1979 by
University Press of America, Inc.™
4710 Auth Place, S.E., Washington, D.C. 20023

All rights reserved
Printed in the United States of America

ISBN: 0-8191-0003-X

TABLE OF CONTENTS

	Page
INTRODUCTION	5
DEDICATION	7
BLACK POLITICS, U.S.A.	9
The Political Stages of the Black Revolution, by Henry A. Bryant	9
Racial Discrimination in the Electoral Process, by Robert B. McKay	13
BLACK INTERNATIONAL POLITICS	31
On Politics, Blacks, and the World, Frankly Speaking, by Henry A. Bryant	31
RACISM IN THE 1970's	47
Black People and the Tyranny of American Law, by Haywood Burns	47
Methodology in Black Studies, by Henry A. Bryant	58
The Attack on Black Studies, by Henry A. Bryant	61
The I.Q. Controversy & Social Science, by Henry A. Bryant	81
Scientific Racism, Its Danger to Social Science, by Henry A. Bryant	87

INTRODUCTION

Henry Bryant is a professor of Black Studies at Laney College in Oakland, California. He earned his B.A. at San Jose University and his M.A. at the same institution. He is one of the new breed of serious Black scholars who is revolutionizing education for Black people in this country. He is a man who is aware that theory and practice should go hand in hand. Black Studies Departments, like the one at Laney College, are making it possible for Black people to seize control of their own destinies, to plan and carry out their own self-help program.

Bryant is a leader in one of the most important Black communities in the country, it is the community in which the Panthers originally developed their ten point program for Black liberation. Oakland is not the largest Black community in the nation; nor are the conditions there as bad as they are, for example, in New York. But, perhaps for these very reasons, Oakland has the strength to put forward leaders, initiate grassroots action, and nurture vital Black education projects. The community colleges of Oakland have produced such men as Bobby Seale and Huey P. Newton.

The students at Laney College know where it is. Most of these students live in the large Black community and all of them know what life has been like there, from West and Market out East along the freeway past the derelict center of town, out to dilapidated housing projects along Bancroft Avenue. Blacks know that the landlords in most of these shacks will never repair them, nor will deprived Black children ever be given their playground. They know that Blacks will never be able to remove themselves from welfare rolls, unless they seize the future for themselves. The students in Henry Bryant's classes are there for a reason, because Blacks have learned that knowledge of oneself precedes the liberation of oneself.

This book was originally conceived out of the necessity of finding something which could be used in both of the author's specialties, mainly politics and Racism, as a supplemental reader for his classes. Most of the articles were written by the author extending over a period from summer 1971 to summer 1976, which makes it contemporary dealing with politics, and racism which is happening right now.

Other articles from outstanding authors have been used to add substance and direction to the book, as a strong effort has been made to analyze the political and the racial concepts as they affect Blacks in the United States and around the world. The book can be of exceptional use as a supplementary reader in any course on Racism, Black American Politics, and Black World Politics, and Black Studies in general.

I wish to thank Ms. Marva Edwards, Ms. Susan McKnight, and Ms. Patricia Nevels, for patiently typing most of the articles for this book. I would also like to thank Dr. Raymond Fellers for his patience and understanding in this book.

                                      Sincerely,

                                      Henry A. Bryant
                                      Instructor, Laney College
                                      June 3, 1976

DEDICATION

I would like to dedicate this book to my loving wife Peggy, my daughter Rehema, and my son Moturi, who shall carry on in my tradition.

The Political Stages of the Black Revolution

Henry Bryant

The contemporary Black Revolution can easily be divided into five distinct political stages: 1) The stage of the boycotts; 2) The stage of the "ins"—which consisted of the sit-ins, the pray-ins, the jail-ins, and the non-violent stage of the revolution; 3) The stage of spontaneous violence, culminating in the revolts in the cities; 4) The stage of Black Power, with its thrust for political power through self-defense, organization, and elections; and, 5) The final and present stage—that of Pan-Africanism, or the international thrust for total justice.

The contemporary Black Revolution in America is said to have begun in the year 1955 with the Rosa Parks incident. On December 5, 1955, Rosa Parks, a Black seamstress from Montgomery, Alabama, decided not to obey the ancient custom which required the "nigger" to move to the back of the bus. Because of this, she was forceably ejected from the bus and arrested. The events which followed are revolutionary history. Martin Luther King, who was initially to come to prominence with the Montgomery Bus Boycott, was elected head of the Montgomery Improvement Association.[1]

Blacks had finally reached their summit of patience. The Parks' incident was the climax of weeks of smoldering sentiment and abusive incidents. A young Black veteran had been clubbed unmercifully by a White bus driver with a money changer. It required numerous stitches to close the wound. The bus driver was fined a meagre $25.00, and set free. A young Black girl had been dragged screaming from a bus, because she had refused to yield her seat to a White patron.

The decision of the Montgomery group was to boycott the bus line. Car pools were organized, and regular pep meetings were held to the sound of deeply moving spirituals and hymns. Skillfully utilizing the mass media, King transformed Montgomery into an international headquarters. Finally on December 21, 1956, after a Federal Court Order, the busses were integrated.

Little Rock, Arkansas

The die was cast. Protest demonstrations began to steamroll. On May 17, 1955, a prayer pilgrimage was held in Washington, D.C.—the largest demonstration of its kind up to that period. In Tuskeegee, Alabama, as a result of acts of the State Legislature which deprived them of municipal votes by placing their homes outside the city limit, Blacks boycotted city stores. In Tallahassee, Florida, a boycott began on April 23, 1956. On September 6, 1956, the National Guard was called out in Sturgis, Kentucky, to put down a riot of Whites, because of the integration of schools there. Then, on September 24, 1957, President Eisenhower startled the nation, and especially the Whites, by ordering Federal troops into Little Rock, Arkansas, to put down threats of a White mob to attack Blacks who were integrating Central High School. The Black Revolution, aimed at reforming racist America through moral fortitude, was now in full swing. However, as with every new thing, the initial effect soon wears off. White America was no longer shocked or morally belittled by the effects of the boycott and the school integration efforts. As the effectiveness of one revolutionary method subsides, it is necessary to find another—thus elevating the Revolution to another stage in order to counter another evil (i.e., discrimination in public accommodations).

The next stage of the Revolution was to begin in an obscure lunch counter on August 19, 1958, in Oklahoma City. Some members of the N.A.A.C.P. Youth Council staged a sit-in. However, the incident received only minor publicity. On February 1, 1960, four students from North Carolina A & T College in Greensboro, North Carolina, sat-in at a dime store. By February 10, the movement had spread to fifteen Southern cities in five states. On February 27, policemen arrested one hundred students in a Nashville sit-in demonstration. During that period of the early 60's, freedom schools for the instruction of participants in the "manly" art of passive resistance were set up. Students were taught how to "roll with the punches," how to cover their mid-section and, most of all, how to take abuse without striking back. The participants were to meet the brute force of the oppressor with the "soul force" of passive resistance. They were to learn to return a curse with a smile, and a blow with contorted muscular actions designed to protect vital body portions from serious injury.

The "ins" were in. Sit-ins were followed by pray-ins, and even jail-ins. The jail-in movement was conceived at Rock Hill, South Carolina, on February 6, 1961, when students refused to pay fines and chose to go to jail instead. During the early 60's, the "freedom riders" began their expeditions into the South under the direction of the Congress of Racial Equality. On May 14, 1961, they were attacked and their busses burned at Anniston, Alabama. Following this, White mobs attacked a group of "freedom riders" at Montgomery, Alabama on May 20, 1961.

Passive resistance tactics predominated until the mid-1960's. Once again the practical effectiveness of this phase of revolution was proving itself ineffective. The oppressors once again adjusted themselves to the situation. With this, came the surfacing of frustration which had lain dormant in the souls of Black people for over four hundred years. White America was going to realize the significance of Malcolm X's statement that a racial powder keg was much more serious than even an atomic bomb.[2]

On July 18, 1964, revolt and insurrection errupted against oppression and degradation. The situation was a simultaneous one. No one had to tell Black people that they were mad at the White establishment. Some Whites have the feeling that White subversives from a White nation (Russia), which is oppressing and exploiting the people of color in its own nation, had to tell Blacks in America to wake up—White America is kicking your behind, so do something about it! Anyone who would believe that revolts in this country involving Black people are Communist-inspired is suffering from considerable delusion. The so-called riots demonstrated that Black people had reached their breaking point. Non-violence was loosing its significance. A new consensus of self-defense was emerging.

In 1965, a revolt occurred in Los Angeles' predominantly Black section of Watts. It began with the arrest of another Black. Once arrested, the Black is well aware of the results—he will probably be beaten in the patrol car on the way to the police station; he will be abused by cowardly, invective-strewn White racists; and, most important, he is usually innocent. The arrest is merely the climax of one constant harassment of a captive people (Black) by the occupying forces of their community (White policemen).

Millions of dollars in property was destroyed—most of it in the Black community. But, so what? Didn't it really belong to the White man? Black men and women could be seen "looting" stores of businessmen who had cheated them with extravagant interest rates on cheap, inferior merchandise and grocery stores who sold rat-infested meat to Blacks for prices three times as high as those in the White community. Over thirty people were

killed; so what? Wouldn't you die anyway? Thousands were jailed; but, didn't Malcolm say that if you were Black you were born in jail?

The scene was to be repeated for the next few years with each revolt growing in its intensity. Newark was to be next—in 1967, its insurrection was of greater severity than Watts. Property damage soared into the millions. The Newark rebellion left twenty-six dead, and one thousand and four (1,004) injured. It had begun on July 11, 1967, and had spent itself by Sunday, July 17, 1967. Black America was bringing restitution to the White Establishment.

Also in 1967, Detroit became the next place of revolt. Here again, the same conditions that had precipitated revolts in Watts, New York, and Newark predominated: unemployment due to racial discrimination, high crime, high school drop-out rates, inferior school systems, and social congestion due to confinement into the Black Ghetto. Detroit was ripe as an apple—and it was picked.

The establishment soon adjusted—in 1968, they had even gone so far as to give Blacks a season. Not only was there a deer season, duck season, Spring, Fall and Winter, but there was now a riot season. It was determined as the "Long Hot Summer." What would the "Nigger Season" bring this year? However, Black people had determined not to take part in this year's festivities. White America anxiously awaited the opening of the season with its "patented answer" to the problem—guns, bullets, armoured personnel carriers, and more. However, the passive assistance movement was over. Nothing could have brought it to a brutal close so shockingly as the murder of Martin Luther King on April 4, 1968.

A new stage of the Revolution was emerging. It was the era of Black Power which was already in action. The term had been conceived by Stokley Carmichael in an atmosphere of militancy during James Meredith's march through Mississippi in 1965. Black Power was to mean many things to many people. To the Whites it was confused with retribution through violence—"get Whitey," and revolution in the White community by Black insurgents. To Black people, its meaning and true significance was clearcut—the right of Black people to control their own destiny.

It spouted the philosophy that Black people were to control the political, social, and economic institutions within their community. The Black community was to develop relevant curriculi, and Blacks were to teach their own people. Black people were to own the stores in the Black community and keep the profits within their community—thereby upgrading it economically.

Black people were to select their own political representatives, and make these representatives responsible to the Black community alone.

Black Power was to witness political organization for the purpose of control. 1967 saw the election of Blacks to noted positions in large cities. Carl Stokes used the power of organization, and the aid of the Black bloc vote, to sweep into the office of Mayor in Cleveland, Ohio. He has since been re-elected. Richard Hatcher used the same mechanism to achieve the same office in Gary, Indiana. He has also been re-elected.

Black Power recognized the necessity of Black people to do something for themselves other than throwing themselves mercilessly into the guns of the White man. It saw Stokley Carmichael stand and proclaim that the major organizations which had led the thrust of the Revolution had to begin to assume responsibility for their own direction; CORE and SNCC had to be taken away from the White liberal. The White liberals departed, and took their money with them. Black people, they insisted, had become too militant.

Black Power saw the rise of militant organizations led by dedicated young men who saw self-defense, and not passive resistance, as the means to survival. Stokley Carmichael concluded that Black people had worked too long from a weak vantage point. What was needed was a thrust towards power. America was not a moral nation, and passive resistance was meant as an appeal to a moral conscience-America had none. Huey P. Newton, Eldridge Cleaver, and Bobby Seale moved the obscure Black Panther Party to national prominence. It became, and remains, a visual symbol of Black people's changing consciousness from passive resistance to freedom—freedom at all costs: through the ballot, the pen, or the bullet.

Black Power saw the development of Black Studies departments at colleges all over the nation. These departments are designed to instruct the total student population about the culture, history, sociology, politics, and anthropology of Black people. They should provide the ideology which preceded the implementation. Ideas do provide the ground rules for action, whether social, political, or economic. Black Studies should demonstrate the Black's role in American history and World history, as well as their cultural accomplishments and contributions, their origins, and their destiny.

Although Black Power still prevails, a new consensus for a broader thrust—an international push—was developing. No longer could Black America isolate itself, but it had to link itself to those nations who suffer a common oppression, have a common heritage, have a common enemy, and seek a common destiny. There were Black people in South America, the Carribbean, Canada, and Africa who were suffering the same fate as Black people in America. A new call for unity, using an old ideology is developing. It is the ideology of Pan-Africanism, which was conceived in 1919 by W.E.B. DuBois. It is an old ideology which has found its place in today's Revolution by referring to Black people uniting all over the Black world for a total thrust to destroy oppression and racism.

The Black Revolution marches on.

1. Lerone Bennett, *Before the Mayflower,* Johnson Publishing Company, p. 59.
2. Malcolm X, *The Ballot or the Bullet,* Speech made in Muslim Mosque in 1964.

Racial Discrimination in the Electoral Process

By ROBERT B. McKAY

ABSTRACT: Nearly a century ago the Supreme Court of the United States acknowledged that the right to vote is "a fundamental political right, because preservative of all rights." A Court thus armed with lofty ideals might have been expected to apply the Fourteenth and Fifteenth Amendments to strike down racially discriminatory restrictions on the franchise that were adopted by many states after the Reconstruction period ended with the Hayes-Tilden Compromise of 1876. However, the Supreme Court largely confined its efforts to rhetoric and for many decades closed its eyes to the use of the white primary, literacy tests, the poll tax, and other devices to deny black citizens the vote. The white primary was at last outlawed in 1944, but Congress did not act until 1957. The Civil Rights Acts of 1957, 1960, and 1964 were well intended but not very effective. The Voting Rights Act of 1965, as amended in 1970, is now the principal vehicle for protection of the franchise against racial discrimination. It forbids literacy tests and other discriminatory tests and devices and requires federal approval of any changes in voting qualifications or procedures in states with a history of voting discrimination.

Robert B. McKay, J.D., Yale Law School, has been Dean of the New York University School of Law since 1967 and a Professor there since 1953. Prior to that he was Assistant and Associate Professor of Law at Emory University (1950–53) and an Attorney for the Department of Justice (1947–50). He was Chairman of the New York State Special Commission on Attica (1971–72) and its presently Chairman of the Citizens Union and Vice-President of the Legal Aid Society of New York. In 1961 he received the Ross Essay Prize of the American Bar Association, and his book, Reapportionment, *was first published in 1965.*

Racial Discrimination in the Electoral Process

OF all the discriminations endured by black citizens of the United States, none has more fully revealed the intent of the white majority to suppress the black minority than the pervasive and long-enduring efforts to limit access to the ballot. Without even the thin pretense of "separate but equal" facilities that long sustained the practice of segregation, racially discriminatory denial of the right to vote has no purpose but to limit control of government to the favored class. The theme persists in South Africa today where denial of the right of franchise to nonwhites is the centerpiece of a system of massive exploitation and suppression of freedom.[1] A measure of the difference between South Africa and the United States is that in this country it has been official policy for more than a century that such discrimination is intolerable. A measure of our own imperfection is the fact that it should have taken so long in the United States to bring practice into line with aspiration, a task still not completely accomplished. What follows is a statement of the effort to perfect the American dream of democracy through freedom of access to the electoral process.[2]

Neither the original Constitution of the United States, as ratified in 1789, nor the Bill of Rights, ratified in 1791, forbade discrimination in the electoral process. Nothing was specified as to the qualifications of voters in federal elections; and in article I, section 2 the states were authorized to fix the qualifications of voters.[3] The same section of the Constitution included an almost explicit invitation to deny the vote at least to those blacks who were slaves, specifying that the apportionment of representatives in Congress should be determined "by adding to the whole Number of free Persons . . . three fifths of all other Persons." This provision was not eliminated until 1868 when the Fourteenth Amendment was ratified.[4]

When the states were given primary responsibility for fixing the qualifications of voters, it was entirely clear that in most states this meant restriction of the franchise to a handful of property owners.[5] It was not until well into the nineteenth century that property qualifications for the exercise of the franchise were largely removed.[6]

---

1. Joel Carlson, "South Africa Today: The Security of the State vs. the Liberty of the Individual." *Human Rights* 2 (1972), p. 125.

2. There are parallel stories to be told of voter discrimination in relation to women and non-English-speaking citizens. But here the emphasis will be on the experience of black citizens.

3. The only limitation on state power to fix voter qualifications in the original Constitution was the proviso in article I, section 4, applicable only to elections for U.S. senators and representatives, that Congress could "make or alter such Regulations." Moreover, until ratification of the Seventeenth Amendment in 1913, U.S. senators were elected by state legislatures rather than by popular election.

4. The franchise was not extended to women as a matter of federal right until 1920, when the Nineteenth Amendment was ratified.

5. When the Constitution was ratified, not more than a quarter of the adult males were entitled to vote. See Albert McKinley, *The Suffrage Franchise in the Thirteen English Colonies in America* (Philadelphia: University of Pennsylvania, 1905), p. 488.

6. In New York State, for example, property qualifications were eliminated for white voters in 1826 for the election of state officials, but not until 1874 for black voters. 1821 Const., art. II, sec. I, as amended in 1826; 1846 Const., art. II, sec. I, as amended in 1874. Other property qualifications for limited purpose elections have been invalidated more recently in *Kramer* v. *Union Free School District No. 15*, 395 U.S. 621 (1969); *Cipriano* v. *City of Houma*, 395 U.S. 701 (1969); and *Phoenix* v. *Kolodziejski*, 399 U.S. 204 (1970). But compare *Gordon* v. *Lance*, 403 U.S. 1 (1971); *Salyer Land Co.* v. *Tulare Water District*, — U.S. — (1973); *Associated Enterprises, Inc.* v. *Toltec Watershed Improvement District*, — U.S. — (1973).

Congress did not attempt in any significant way to alter state voting qualifications for senatorial, congressional, vice-presidential, and presidential elections until the Voting Rights Act Amendments of 1970 lowered the voting age to eighteen.[7]

Nearly a century ago the Supreme Court acknowledged the central importance of equal access to the franchise, noting that the right to vote is "a fundamental political right, because preservative of all rights."[8] Ironically, however, that statement was dictum in a case involving the right of aliens to equal employment rights.

Although the franchise was accorded verbal protection by constitutional amendment, by statute, and by judicial utterance, the reality was very different in the late nineteenth century and during the early decades of the twentieth century. However familiar that story of unfulfilled promise and effective disfranchisement of millions of citizens, summary restatement is necessary here as a prelude to a review of more recent efforts to overcome long-standing patterns of discrimination.

Before the Civil War racial discrimination in exercise of the franchise was not limited to slaves. Free black citizens were also disfranchised in all except five New England states.[9] At the conclusion of the Civil War, the Thirteenth Amendment was quickly approved by Congress and ratified by the states; but it was not clear whether its straightforward prohibition of slavery and involuntary servitude was sufficient authorization for the body of civil rights legislation that a Reconstruction-minded Congress desired to enact. Even though Congress was able to pass the 1866 Civil Rights Act[10] over the veto of President Andrew Johnson, some doubted the adequacy of the constitutional base. The more explicit Fourteenth Amendment, ratified two years later, was "undoubtedly directed at the Black Codes in the southern states . . . restricting the right of nonwhites to hold property, enter into contracts, and to have access to the courts."[11] But it was not clear, even in the minds of some proponents, that the amendment gave the right to vote to black citizens.[12] Accordingly, after the election of 1868, in which the temporizing policies of President Johnson were decisively repudiated, Congress went on to the Fifteenth Amendment, which was submitted to the states in February 1869 and ratified by the required number of states in March 1870. This allowed enactment of the Enforcement Act in 1870,[13] fixing penalties for acts in limitation of the franchise by intimidation, force, or bribery, and further legislation in 1871 to strengthen the 1870 act,[14] plus a criminal statute —the so-called Ku Klux Klan Act— authorizing the president to suspend the privilege of the writ of habeas corpus in the process of suppressing organizations charged with conspiring to deprive citizens of their rights.[15]

---

7. 84 Stat. 314, 318 (1970). When Congress sought to lower the voting age to eighteen for state elections as well as federal, the Supreme Court read section 4 of article I to permit that result as to federal elections, but to deny that power as to state elections because of section 2 of article I. *Oregon v. Mitchell*, 400 U.S. 112 (1970). The Twenty-sixth Amendment, ratified in 1971, lowered the voting age for all elections, state as well as federal, to eighteen.

8. *Yick Wo v. Hopkins*, 118 U.S. 356, 370 (1886).

9. See *Oregon v. Mitchell*, 400 U.S. 112, 156 (1970) (Harlan, J., concurring and dissenting).

10. 14 Stat. 27 (1866).

11. Earl Warren, "Notre Dame Law School Civil Rights Lectures," *Notre Dame Lawyer* 48 (1972), pp. 14, 32.

12. Ibid.

13. 16 Stat. 140 (1870).

14. 16 Stat. 433 (1871).

15. 17 Stat. 13 (1871).

Nation's mood changes

The mood of the nation changed quickly, however; and the ardor of the Reconstructionists was soon thwarted in a variety of ways. During the balance of the nineteenth century, Congress enacted only one further piece of civil rights legislation, the Civil Rights Act of 1875,[16] which was largely emasculated by the Supreme Court in 1883 in the *Civil Rights Cases*.[17] Meanwhile, however, the Court had acknowledged that the three post–Civil War amendments had

> one pervading purpose . . . lying at the foundation of each, and without which none of them would have been suggested; we mean the freedom of the slave race, the security and firm establishment of that freedom, and the protection of the newly-made freeman and citizen from the oppression of those who had formerly exercised unlimited dominion over him.[18]

But in the same case—where the issue was property rights, not individual rights—the Court so narrowed the interpretation of the privileges and immunities clause of the Fourteenth Amendment that it has never since been useful as a protection against racial or other discriminations.[19]

The Enforcement Act was not received sympathetically in the Supreme Court. In *United States v. Cruikshank*[20] and in *United States v. Reese*[21] the Court voided some provisions of the statute and read others restrictively, with the practical result of making the act inoperative.[22]

The judiciary was not alone in its hostility to the Reconstruction legislation and the attitudes that prompted those laws. The nation's enthusiasm for vindication of Negro rights cooled quickly; and the executive and legislative branches were entirely willing to cooperate. In 1876, the same year as the *Cruikshank* and *Reese* decisions, the Reconstruction period was effectively ended when the Hayes-Tilden Compromise accomplished the withdrawal of federal troops from the South.[23] After a brief interval of relative freedom in exercise of the franchise and in other respects, white dominance again became a fact of life in large areas of the nation.[24]

By the early years of the twentieth century, access to the ballot was generally restricted in the South—and limi-

---

16. 18 Stat. 335 (1875). For a discussion of the fate of the civil rights legislation of the Reconstruction period, see Eugene Gressman, "The Unhappy History of Civil Rights Legislation," *Michigan Law Review* 50 (1952), p. 1323. The next civil rights legislation was in 1957, discussed below at notes 66–68.

17. 109 U.S. 3 (1883).

18. *Slaughter-House Cases*, 83 U.S. 36, 71 (16 Wall. 1873). See also *Minor v. Happersett*, 88 U.S. 162 (21 Wall. 1875).

19. Id. at 74–80.

20. 92 U.S. 542 (1876).

21. 92 U.S. 214 (1876).

22. In *Reese* the Court invalidated provisions of the statute on the ground that the statutory language was overbroad, permitting punishment of conduct not based on race. Other provisions of the civil rights legislation of this period were invalidated on the ground that the statutory language was too broad, reaching private action not coupled with state action. See *United States v. Harris*, 106 U.S. 629 (1883); *Civil Rights Cases*, 109 U.S. 3 (1883); *Baldwin v. Franks*, 120 U.S. 678 (1878); *James v. Bowman*, 190 U.S. 127 (1903).

23. For discussion of these events, see J. H. Franklin, *Reconstruction: After the Civil War* (Chicago: University of Chicago Press, 1961); C. Vann Woodward, *The Strange Career of Jim Crow* (New York: Oxford University Press, 1957); C. Vann Woodward, *Reunion and Reaction: The Compromise of 1876 and the End of Reconstruction* (Boston: Little, Brown, 1951).

24. For an extraordinarily vivid judicial recounting of the experiences in a single state, see the opinion of Judge John Minor Wisdom in *United States v. Louisiana*, 225 F. Supp. 353 (E.D. La. 1963), aff'd, 380 U.S. 145 (1965).

tations were not unknown in the North. All of the original Confederate States adopted the poll tax, and seven enacted revisions of the so-called Mississippi Solution, in which reliance was placed on poll taxes, literacy and "understanding" tests, and residency requirements designed to assure disfranchisement of black voters. In *Williams* v. *Mississippi*[25] the Supreme Court upheld the Mississippi program in 1898 in a strikingly narrow reading of the apparently explicit language of the Fifteenth Amendment.

The other principal instrument of disfranchisement was the white primary. By 1915 white primaries controlled access to the ballot in all southern states.[26] As Professor Woodward has observed,

if the Negroes did learn to read, or acquire sufficient property, and remember to pay the poll tax and to keep the receipt on file, they could even then be tripped by the final hurdle devised for them—the white primary.[27]

The courts were of little assistance. The white primary was not invalidated until 1944.[28] Redistricting to deny effective participation in the electoral process was not forbidden until 1960.[29] Early in the twentieth century the Supreme Court had denied the use of its equity power to protect purely political rights such as the right to vote;[30] and when the black plaintiffs sued at law, the Court denied recovery on technical grounds.[31] The path to judicial relief was slow, and the assistance of Congress came even later. The judicial and legislative developments, although of course related, are separately described below.

JUDICIAL VINDICATION OF THE FRANCHISE

White primaries

The right to vote free of racial discrimination received little assistance from the federal courts until the third decade of the twentieth century, when the Supreme Court held invalid a state law that explicitly excluded Negroes from participation in Texas Democratic primaries.[32] Thus rebuffed, the state legislature gave the party's executive committee the power to fix membership qualifications. The not surprising racial exclusion that followed was also found unconstitutional.[33] Un-

---

25. 170 U.S. 213 (1878). See Woodward, *The Strange Career of Jim Crow* (rev. ed. 1968), pp. 84–85.
26. Woodward, *The Strange Career of Jim Crow* (rev. ed. 1968), pp. 85–97.
27. Ibid., p 84.
28. *Smith* v. *Allwright*, 321 U.S. 649 (1955), overruling *Grovey* v. *Townsend*, 295 U.S. 45 (1935), in which the Court had upheld a racial exclusion by the Texas Democratic Convention.
29. *Gomillion* v. *Lightfoot*, 364 U.S. 339 (1960). But compare *Wright* v. *Rockefeller*, 376 U.S. 52 (1964), rejecting a claim that congressional districts in New York City were racially gerrymandered.
30. *Giles* v. *Harris*, 189 U.S. 475 (1903). Mr. Justice Oliver Wendell Holmes in effect acknowledged the racial discrimination, but thought the courts powerless to act. His words, which now sound archaic, were long accepted as the justification for judicial—and even legislative—impotence. He said: "Equity cannot undertake now, any more than it has in the past, to enforce political rights. . . . The bill imports that the great mass of the white population intends to keep the blacks from voting. To meet such an intent something more than ordering the plaintiff's name to be inscribed upon the lists of 1902 will be needed. . . . Unless we are prepared to supervise the voting in that state by officers of the court, it seems to us that all the plaintiff could get from equity would be an empty form." Id. at 488.
31. *Giles* v. *Teasly*, 193 U.S. 146 (1904).
32. *Nixon* v. *Herndon*, 273 U.S. 536 (1924).
33. *Nixon* v. *Condon*, 286 U.S. 73 (1932). Interestingly, both *Nixon* cases were grounded on the equal protection of the laws clause of the Fourteenth Amendment rather than on the more explicit wording of the Fifteenth

abashed by these rulings, the state convention of the Texas Democratic Party developed its own rules of racial exclusion, which survived constitutional challenge in *Grovey v. Townsend*,[34] a 1935 case that was not overruled until 1944 in *Smith v. Allwright*.[35] In the latter case the Court relied on an intervening decision in *United States* v. *Classic*,[36] which held that article I, section 4 of the Constitution authorizes congressional control of primaries "where the primary is by law made an integral part of the election machinery."[37]

The white primary was not dead even then. Bearing in mind the literal words of *Smith* v. *Allwright*, but none of its significance, proponents of discrimination attempted other evasions. Lower federal courts invalidated efforts to preserve the white primary by repealing all state laws dealing with the subject, leaving the fixing of racial restrictions entirely to the "private" party organizations. In *Rice v. Elmore*[38] the Fourth Circuit concluded: "Having undertaken to perform an important function relating to the exercise of sovereignty by the people, [the party] may not violate the fundamental principles laid down by the Constitution for its exercise."[39]

The final attempt to preserve the white primary arose out of the "preprimary" elections of the Jaybird Democratic Association in Texas, which was a "voluntary club" of white Democrats. Since candidates winning the Jaybird preprimary contests usually ran unopposed in the Democratic primaries, the Supreme Court concluded that the Fifteenth Amendment was violated.[40]

In all these cases, and others now to be mentioned, the federal courts were performing the essentially negative role assigned them by the Fourteenth and Fifteenth Amendments. The Supreme Court had long before said—and had not since denied—that the Constitution "does not confer the right of suffrage upon anyone."[41] As recently as 1959 the Court stated that the right to vote referred to in section 2 of the Fourteenth Amendment was a right "established by the laws and constitution of the State."[42]

Despite the decades-long dominance of the view that the political process was largely beyond the reach of legislative and judicial supervision, almost from the first a more affirmative note was sometimes expressed by the Supreme Court. In *Ex parte Yarbrough*,[43] the Court noted that the Fifteenth Amendment "clearly shows that the right of suffrage was considered to be of supreme importance to the national government, and was not intended to be left within the exclusive control of the States."[44] The Court recognized that the words of negation also carried the seeds of affirmation, the confirming of a right to vote. Conceding that the

---

Amendment. Although reliance on equal protection was certainly logical enough, the Court did not again base its judgment on the Fourteenth Amendment in a voting case until the legislative apportionment cases in the 1960s. See *Baker v. Carr*, 369 U.S. 186 (1962); *Gray* v. *Sanders*, 372 U.S. 368 (1963); *Reynolds* v. *Sims*, 377 U.S. 533 (1964).

34. 295 U.S. 45 (1935).
35. 321 U.S. 649 (1944).
36. 313 U.S. 299 (1941).
37. Id. at 318.
38. 165 F. 2d 387 (4th Cir. 1947), cert. denied, 333 U.S. 875 (1948).
39. Id., 165 F. 2d at 391. See also *Baskin* v. *Brown*, 174 F. 2d 391 (4th Cir. 1949).

40. *Terry* v. *Adams*, 345 U.S. 461 (1953).
41. *Pope* v. *Williams*, 193 U.S. 621, 633 (1904).
42. *Lassiter* v. *Northampton County Board of Elections*, 360 U.S. 45, 51 (1959), quoting from *McPherson* v. *Blacker*, 146 U.S. 1, 39 (1892).
43. 110 U.S. 651 (1884).
44. Id. at 664. See also *Ex Parte Siebold*, 100 U.S. 371 (1880); *Neal* v. *Delaware*, 103 U.S. 370, 389 (1881).

Fifteenth Amendment had originally been construed as giving "no affirmative right to the colored man to vote," and as having been "designed primarily to prevent discrimination against him," the Court for the first time saw that "under some circumstances it may operate as the immediate source of a right to vote." [45]

What was long thought to be the limited potential for judicial intervention in protection of the right of franchise against racially motivated restriction is emphasized by the fact that there are only three provisions in the Constitution of the United States that "deny plenary and exclusive power to the States to determine voting requirements and give special protection to a citizen against discrimination in the electoral process." [46] The Fourteenth and Fifteenth Amendments offer grounds for judicial intervention for violation of their prohibitions as well as a basis for congressional action to enforce through appropriate legislation. Article I, section 4, on the other hand, provides no basis for judicial intervention in the absence of congressional action.

Literacy tests

The most important—and most explicit—is the Fifteenth Amendment:

The right of citizens of the United States to vote shall not be denied or abridged by the United States or by any state on account of race, color, or previous condition of servitude.

The phrase "on account of race" has made it possible to strike down even laws fair on their face that in fact concealed devices of a racially discriminatory nature. The promised availability of the Fifteenth Amendment as an affirmative instrument in vindication of the franchise was, however, long delayed. Literacy tests were upheld against a claim of scarcely disguised racial application.[47] In fact, literacy tests were not finally eliminated until the Voting Rights Act Amendments of 1970[48] barred the use of such tests in all elections, state and national, for a five-year period, on a congressional finding that literacy tests had been used to discriminate against voters on account of their color in violation of the Fourteenth and Fifteenth Amendments. This congressional move to enforce the provisions of those two amendments was unanimously upheld by the Court in *Oregon* v. *Mitchell*.[49]

Poll Taxes

Poll taxes proved similarly difficult to challenge on grounds of racially discriminatory purpose or effect. The Court was unanimous in 1937 in upholding a Georgia poll tax applicable to men between the ages of twenty-one

---

45. 110 U.S. at 665.
46. *United States* v. *Louisiana*, 225 F. Supp. 353, 358 (E.D. La. 1963), aff'd, 380 U.S. 145 (1965).
47. *Williams* v. *United States*, 170 U.S. 213, 220 (1898). In 1959, in *Lassiter* v. *Northampton County Board of Elections*, 360 U.S. 45 (1959), the Court would go no further than to acknowledge that "a literacy test, fair on its face, may not be employed to perpetuate that discrimination which the Fifteenth Amendment was designed to uproot." Id. at 45. The Court gave as an example of that kind of discrimination the case of *Davis* v. *Schnell*, 81 F. Supp. 872 (S.D. Ala.), aff'd, 336 U.S. 933 (1949), in which the test was the citizen's ability to "understand and explain" a provision of the Constitution. That case was a forerunner of *Louisiana* v. *United States*, 380 U.S. 145 (1965), more fully discussed below at notes 57–60.
48. 84 Stat. 314 (1870). See also section 4(e) of the Voting Rights Act of 1965, denying the use of literacy-in-English tests in certain circumstances. 79 Stat. 437, 439 (1965). This provision was upheld as the basis for striking down the English literacy test applied in New York State to exclude certain Spanish-speaking citizens from voting. *Katzenbach* v. *Morgan*, 384 U.S. 641 (1966).
49. 400 U.S. 112 (1970).

and sixty and to women only if they should register to vote.[50] When the poll tax at last fell in 1966, the invalidation was not for reasons of racial discrimination on the face of the Virginia statute there at issue, or as applied, but because the equal protection clause of the Fourteenth Amendment was violated by a provision that "makes the affluence of the voter or payment of any fee an electoral standard."[51] But there were strong dissents even to that proposition, including Justice Hugo Black's insistence that the poll tax could be abolished by Congress pursuant to its authority under section 5 of the Fourteenth Amendment, but not by the judiciary on its own.[52] Ultimately, the Twenty-fourth Amendment was adopted to proscribe the poll tax in all federal elections, and by 1966 all but four states had abolished the poll tax in state elections.[53]

Other discriminatory devices

Discrimination at the polls was not limited to the white primary, literacy tests, and poll taxes. Other devices, even more frankly racial, included the notorious "grandfather" clauses in state election laws and the requirements that applicants for voter registration be able to "interpret" provisions of state constitutions or statutes. Even these remarkably candid devices of racial discrimination long escaped successful challenge.

The grandfather clause was an ingenious solution to an embarrassing problem for the dominant white community. A literacy test would, to be sure, deny most black citizens the vote at the turn of the century; but, if fairly applied, the test would also eliminate many white citizens. Hence, in a number of states white voters were exempted from the literacy test by establishing that their grandfathers had voted, while blacks were excluded because their grandfathers had been nonvoting slaves. Not until 1915 was this pernicious device struck down in *Guinn* v. *United States*,[54] invalidating an amendment to the Oklahoma Constitution that exempted from the literacy test all persons entitled to vote on January 1, 1866, and those whose ancestors were entitled to vote on that date—before ratification of the Fourteenth or Fifteenth Amendment.

Except for the white primary cases discussed above, there were few other cases between 1915 and the Civil Rights Act of 1957 in which the federal courts intervened to protest against continuing racial discrimination in the exercise of the franchise. Only *Lane* v. *Wilson*,[55] in which the Court forbade continued use of unreasonable procedural barriers erected against the vote, is of any significance. And that case may be remembered more for the aphorism of Mr. Justice Felix Frankfurter than for any vital contribution to doctrine or

50. *Breedlove* v. *Suttles*, 302 U.S. 277 (1937).
51. *Harper* v. *Virginia Board of Elections*, 383 U.S. 663, 666 (1966). See also *Carrington* v. *Rash*, 380 U.S. 89 (1965)—striking down a Texas constitutional provision denying the vote to any member of the armed forces who moved to the state during his military service; *Dunn* v. *Blumstein*, 405 U.S. 330 (1972)—striking down Tennessee's one-year residence requirement for voting. But compare *McDonald* v. *Board of Election Commissioners*, 394 U.S. 802 (1969)—upholding an Illinois statute denying absentee ballots to individuals detained in jail awaiting trial; the classification, said the Court, was not based on race or wealth and was not shown to have impaired the right to vote (only the right to receive absentee ballots).
52. 383 U.S. at 670 (Black, J., dissenting).
53. Id. at 680 (Harlan, J., dissenting).

54. 238 U.S. 347 (1915). See also *Myers* v. *Anderson*, 238 U.S. 368 (1915); *Lane* v. *Wilson*, 307 U.S. 268 (1939).
55. 307 U.S. 268 (1939).

practice. His memorable phrase was that the Fifteenth Amendment was intended to nullify "sophisticated as well as simple-minded modes of discrimination."[56]

Louisiana v. United States

Apart from the white primary cases, the most significant judicial contribution to the protection of the franchise from racial distortion was the decision in *Louisiana v. United States*.[57] The case involved the so-called interpretation test for voter registration which had long been available in Louisiana as a means to defeat registration of black citizens who stubbornly overcame all other barriers to the vote. The provision was written into the state constitution in 1921 after the grandfather clause was invalidated; and it was widely used in the 1950s after the white primary was held unconstitutional. In 1960 the state constitution was amended to require an applicant to "be able to understand and give a reasonable interpretation" of any provision of the Louisiana or United States Constitution. The provision was attacked for violation of the Fourteenth and Fifteenth Amendments and section 1971 of title 42 of the United States Code. Judge John Wisdom, writing for the three-judge federal district court, examined the history carefully; and he demonstrated convincingly that the test was designed to disfranchise black voters and was administered with the same unacceptable objective. He wrote:

[T]his wall, built to bar Negroes from access to the franchise, must come down. The understanding clause or interpretation test is *not* a literacy requirement. . . . [I]t is evident that the test is a sophisticated scheme to disfranchise Negroes. The test is unconstitutional as written and administered.[58]

The Supreme Court was equally explicit in affirming the judgment of the district court. Although violation of the Civil Rights Act of 1960 was alleged, it was apparent that the force of the Fourteenth and Fifteenth Amendments was entirely adequate for the task at hand. Mr. Justice Black, for a unanimous Court, stated:

This is not a test but a trap, sufficient to stop even the most brilliant man on his way to the voting booth. The cherished right of people in a country like ours to vote cannot be obliterated by the use of laws like this, which leave the voting fate of a citizen to the passing whim or impulse of an individual registrar.[59]

Although the district court and the Supreme Court found in the Fourteenth and Fifteenth Amendments adequate basis for invalidation of the challenged provisions of Louisiana law, the additional allegation of violation of the Civil Rights Act of 1960 was useful in the framing of a decree to prevent evasion of the judicial mandate. After the suit was filed, but before decision in the district court, Louisiana had already adopted a new voter-qualification test, requiring each applicant for registration to answer correctly four to six multiple-choice questions on one of ten cards drawn by the applicant. The district court did not pass on the validity of the new test, but took it into consideration in formulating the decree. The court found that past discrimina-

---

56. Id. at 275.
57. 380 U.S. 145 (1965).
58. *United States v. Louisiana*, 225 F. Supp. 353, 356 (E.D. La. 1963).
59. *Louisiana v. United States*, 380 U.S. 145, 153 (1965). More than fifteen years earlier a similar provision in Alabama had been invalidated in *Davis v. Schnell*, 81 F. Supp. 872 (S.D. Ala.), aff'd, 336 U.S. 933 (1949); but the "interpretation and understanding" device was not decisively excised until the 1965 decision in *Louisiana v. United States*.

tion against black applicants had reduced their number of registered voters, while the number of white voters was increasing. Accordingly, to allow application of the new test only to new applicants without retesting those already registered would be to disadvantage all those required to take the more vigorous test. Accordingly, the district court ordered postponement of the new test in the affected parishes until a complete reregistration of voters was instituted so that, as the Supreme Court noted in agreement, "the new test will apply alike to all or to none."[60]

With the decision in *Louisiana* v. *United States, supra,* the courts had gone about as far as they were likely to go in their essentially negative role of reacting to and invalidating the more blatant forms of voter discrimination on racial lines. Federal courts had often indicated the potentiality, and indeed the need, for legislation pursuant to the Fourteenth and Fifteenth Amendments to make possible the next step: affirmative support for voter registration and effective use of the ballot. That is the subject of the following section, in which will be related the successes and failures of legislation enacted by Congress between 1957 and 1971.

Congress Acts to Extend the Franchise

Interest in protection of the rights of blacks to vote following the Civil War was brief. The Enforcement Act of 1870[61] made it a crime for public officers and private persons to obstruct exercise of the right to vote. In 1871 the statute was amended[62] to provide for detailed federal supervision of the electoral process, from registration to the certification of returns. But enthusiasm for the venture soon waned, enforcement became spotty,[63] and most civil rights laws were repealed in 1894.[64] Meanwhile, beginning as early as 1890, a number of states began to use tests designed to deny the franchise to their black citizens.[65] Congress made no attempt to restrain these discriminatory practices, and efforts to seek judicial intervention were few and not very successful. Astonishingly, it was not until 1957 that Congress again attempted to protect the democratic heritage of millions of citizens against the most blatant abuses. The Civil Rights Act of 1957[66] authorized the attorney general to seek injunctions against public and private interference with the right to vote on racial grounds. But the enforcement provisions proved cumbersome and evasion relatively easy.[67] Probably the most important contributions of the 1957 Act were the creation

---

60. 380 U.S. at 155. On the remedies question, compare *Gaston County* v. *United States,* 395 U.S. 385 (1969).
61. 16 Stat. 140 (1870).
62. 16 Stat. 433 (1871).
63. *South Carolina* v. *Katzenbach,* 383 U.S. 301, 310 (1966).
64. 28 Stat. 36 (1894). By 1957 only a brief general provision, derived from the 1870 Act, remained applicable to voting rights [42 U.S.C. sec. 1971(a)(1)]: "All citizens of the United States who are otherwise qualified to vote at any election by the people in any State . . . shall be entitled and allowed to vote at all such elections, without distinction of race, color, or previous condition of servitude; any constitution, law, custom, usage or regulation of any State . . . or by or under its authority, to the contrary notwithstanding."
65. See discussion at notes 23–26 below. See also *South Carolina* v. *Katzenbach,* 383 U.S. 301, 310–12 (1966).
66. 71 Stat. 634 (1957). The 1957 Act drew heavily upon the recommendations in the 1947 Report of the President's Committee on Civil Rights, To Secure These Rights.
67. Although the Civil Rights Act of 1957 was upheld, the frustrations of enforcement are clear in the validating decision. *United States* v. *Raines,* 362 U.S. 17 (1960). See also *United States* v. *Thomas,* 362 U.S. 58 (1960); *Hannah* v. *Larche,* 363 U.S. 420 (1960).

of the U.S. Commission on Civil Rights and the establishment of a Civil Rights Division in the Department of Justice. The Commission has not only provided significant information on progress—and lack of progress—in the entire area of civil rights; it has also served as conscience for the public in general and for government in particular.[68] The Civil Rights Division provided a vehicle in the Department of Justice for much of the significant litigation for the protection of civil rights.

The Civil Rights Act of 1960[69] added perfecting amendments that permitted the joinder of states as party defendants, gave the attorney general access to local voting records, and authorized courts to register voters in areas of systematic discrimination. Title I of the Civil Rights Act of 1964[70] expedited the hearing of voting cases before three-judge courts and outlawed some of the tactics still being used to disqualify black voters from participation in federal elections. Despite conscientious application of each remedy provided by an ever-hopeful Congress, the results in terms of voter registration were disappointing[71]; and resistance remained strong in many areas. Only 23 percent of the voting age blacks were registered in the nearly fifty counties in which the Department of Justice had brought law suits between 1957 and 1964.[72]

In response to the continuing difficulties in the way of voter registration, President Lyndon Johnson, on January 4, 1965, proposed in his State of the Union Message that "we eliminate every remaining obstacle to the right and the opportunity to vote."[73] Two months later, on March 7, 1965, civil rights marchers, who sought to dramatize their appeal for the vote by marching from Selma to Montgomery, Alabama were attacked by Alabama law enforcement officers. A week later the President appeared before a special session of Congress to urge the prompt enactment of voting legislation. "No law we now have on the books," he said, "can ensure the right to vote when local officials are determined to deny it."[74]

Voting Rights Act of 1965

After extensive debate the Administration's proposal was modified, approved, and signed by the President on August 6, 1965. The Voting Rights Act of 1965 sought to reach and prevent discrimination in a variety of ways. Central to the scheme was the formula in section 4(b)–(d) defining the states and political subdivisions to which the new remedies would apply. As a first remedy section 4(a) provided for the suspension of literacy tests and similar voting qualifications in the areas within the Act's coverage for a period of five years from the last occurrence

---

68. For a discussion of the contribution of the Commission, see Earl Warren, "Notre Dame Civil Rights Lectures," *Notre Dame Lawyer* 48 (1972), pp. 14, 43–47.
69. 74 Stat. 86 (1960).
70. 78 Stat. 241 (1964).
71. The number of blacks registered to vote in the eleven southern states rose from an estimated 1,238,038 in 1956 to 2,174,000 or 43.3 percent of the voting age black population in 1964. See Margaret Price, *The Negro and the Ballot in the South* (Atlanta: Southern Regional Council, 1959), p. 9; and 1959 Report of the Commission on Civil Rights (Washington, D. C.: U.S. Government Printing Office, 1959), p. 110. See also "Voting Rights: A Case Study of Madison Parish, Louisiana," *University of Chicago Law Review* 38 (1971), pp. 726–51; Sen. Rept. No. 162, Part 3, 89th Cong., 1st sess., *Joint Statement of Individual Views re S. 1564, The Voting Rights Act of 1965*.

72. United States Commission on Civil Rights, *The Voting Rights Act: The First Months* (Washington, D.C., 1965), p. 9.
73. 111 Cong. Rec. 28 (daily ed., Jan. 4, 1965).
74. 111 Cong. Rec. 4924 (daily ed., March 15, 1965).

of substantial voting discrimination.[75] Section 5 prescribed a second remedy, the suspension of all new voting regulations pending review by federal authorities to determine whether their use would perpetuate voting discrimination. The third remedy, in sections 6, 7, 9, and 13, provided for the assignment of federal examiners by the attorney general to list qualified applicants who would thereafter be entitled to vote in all elections. A related provision in section 8 authorized the appointment of federal poll-watchers in places to which federal examiners were assigned. Section 10(d) excused those made eligible to vote in sections of the country covered by section 4(b) of the Act from paying accumulated past poll taxes for state and local elections. Section 12(e) provided for balloting by persons denied access to the polls in areas where federal examiners had been appointed.

In addition to these central provisions, the Act provided a number of subsidiary remedies for special problems, including limitations on the franchise in other parts of the country. Section 2, for example, broadly prohibited the use of voting rules to abridge exercise of the franchise on racial grounds anywhere in the nation. Section 4(e) excused citizens educated in American schools conducted in a foreign

TABLE 1—Percent of Nonwhite Registration

State	Prior to 1965	Spring–Summer 1968
Alabama	19.3	51.6
Arkansas	40.4	62.8
Florida	51.2	63.6
Georgia	27.4	52.6
Louisiana	31.6	58.9
Mississippi	6.7	59.8
North Carolina	46.8	51.3
South Carolina	37.3	51.2
Tennessee	69.5	71.7
Texas	53.1[a]	61.6
Virginia	38.3	55.6

[a] Percentages by race were not available.

language from having to take English-language literacy tests. And other sections provided civil and criminal sanctions for interference with the exercise of rights guaranteed by the Act.

The success of the 1965 Act is demonstrated in at least two ways: first, by the dramatic increase in the proportion of nonwhite voting registration in the period immediately following enactment of the legislation; and second, by the intensity of the attacks on its constitutionality and by the substantial effort to prevent renewal in 1970.

The fact of success is supported in Table 1, showing the significant gains made in the southern states.[76] Opposition to the 1965 Act was expressed in the congressional debates over renewal of the Act as its expiration date neared in 1970. However, the Act was ultimately renewed in 1970 and even strengthened in minor ways.[77] The Act also survived early tests of its constitutionality in *South Carolina* v. *Katzen-*

---

75. Section 4 was made applicable to any state or political subdivision where any such test or device was in effect in November 1964 and where less than 50 percent of the black voting age population had voted in the November 1964 election. The following states were originally covered by the Voting Rights Act of 1965: Alabama, Georgia, Louisiana, Mississippi, South Carolina, Virginia, and twenty-six counties in North Carolina. Under the 1970 amendments the following areas were covered: nine counties in Arizona, two in California, three in New York, one in Wyoming, and four election districts in Alaska. "Voting Rights," *Civil Rights Digest* 31, (December 1971).

76. *Political Participation: 1968 Report of the United States Commission on Civil Rights* (Washington, D.C.: U.S. GPO, 1968), pp. 12–13.

77. 84 Stat. 314 (1970).

bach[78] and *Katzenbach* v. *Morgan*.[79] Additional questions have been resolved in subsequent Supreme Court decisions,[80] while other issues still await final answers. The issues already resolved and those that remain under judicial inquiry, involve important questions of federalism and the extent of federal power that may be exercised by the legislative, executive, and judicial branches of the national government. These issues will be examined in the remaining portions of this paper.

South Carolina v. Katzenbach

South Carolina v. *Katzenbach* is the most important of the cases that arose out of the Voting Rights Act of 1965 because in that litigation the Supreme Court sustained the Act in all its principal provisions. Congress had acted boldly and inventively in defining the coverage of the Act, suspending literacy tests and other suspected devices in the covered areas, and in forbidding unapproved changes in voting qualifications or procedures in effect on November 1, 1964. Thus, at one stroke the new legislation sought to outlaw existing devices for voter discrimination and to discourage circumvention of the Act by the creation of new techniques of discrimination.

The legislative thrust was both more far reaching and more particularized in its impact than anything previously attempted. The affected areas argued that Congress could do no more under the authority of section 2 of the Fifteenth Amendment than forbid violations of that amendment in general terms, leaving to courts the task of fashioning specific remedies applicable to particular localities where abuse was found. The Court answered the contention in sweeping terms with the direct statement that "Congress is not circumscribed by any such artificial rules under section 2 of the Fifteenth Amendment."[81] The Court recognized that the congressional formula was at best blunt and imperfect, omitting from coverage some areas in which voter discrimination occurred, while including some in which there was no proven discrimination. Nonetheless, the Court concluded that Congress had acted within permissible limits, particularly since relief from coverage could be secured upon an adequate showing of nondiscrimination in exercise of the franchise.[82] The decision is significant not only for its validation of the new methods for attacking voting discrimination, but also for the expansive interpretation there confirmed of the flexibility of the affirmative powers entrusted to Congress in enforcing the negative provisions of the Fifteenth Amendment.

Katzenbach v. Morgan

Katzenbach v. *Morgan*[83] dealt with a narrower aspect of the Voting Rights Act but was no less sweeping in its affirmation of congressional authority, in this case pursuant to section 5 of the Fourteenth Amendment. The case involved the validity of section 4(e) of

---

78. 383 U.S. 301 (1966).
79. 384 U.S. 641 (1966). See also *Cardona* v. *Power*, 384 U.S. 672 (1966).
80. *Allen* v. *State Board of Elections*, 393 U.S. 544 (1969); *Gaston County, North Carolina* v. *United States*, 395 U.S. 285 (1969); *Perkins* v. *Matthews*, 400 U.S. 379 (1971).
81. 383 U.S. 301, 327 (1969).
82. Only Mr. Justice Black dissented, and he disagreed only with the Court's approval of section 5 relating to the suspension of tests and devices in covered areas except with the approval of the attorney general or the federal district court in the District of Columbia. He believed that section unconstitutional in providing for a judicial proceeding in the absence of a justiciable case or controversy and for intrusion into the power of the states in requiring approval by federal authorities for the enactment of voter qualification laws.
83. 384 U.S. 641 (1966).

the Voting Rights Act of 1965, which in effect eliminated the literacy-in-English test as administered in New York State for individuals who had successfully completed the sixth grade in a school accredited by the Commonwealth of Puerto Rico in which the instruction was not in English. The Court acknowledged that literacy tests had not at that time been held to violate the equal protection clause; but, that was found to be no bar. This was "appropriate" legislation "plainly adapted" to furthering the aims of the equal protection clause.[84]

In combination, the *South Carolina* and *Morgan* cases offer Congress a strong arsenal of powers from which to choose in providing effective affirmative enforcement of the negatively worded provisions in the substantive clauses of the Fourteenth and Fifteenth Amendments. Without recognition of that principle, the drive to end discrimination in the exercise of voting rights would have been greatly handicapped.

Allen v. State Board of Elections

After this strong initial thrust, the next series of cases may not have seemed as difficult, but they, too, are important. *Allen* v. *State Board of Elections*[85] involved applications of section 5 of the Voting Rights Act of 1965 in which the Court held that four changes in state election provisions—three in Mississippi and one in Virginia—were subject to the approval requirements of section 5. Under the Mississippi amendments (1) county supervisors were to be elected at large rather than by districts; (2) superintendents of education in certain counties were made appointive rather than elective; and (3) ballot-access requirements for independent candidates running in general elections were stiffened. Virginia had adopted new procedures for casting write-in ballots which had the effect of barring the use of printed labels by illiterate voters.

The Court concluded that section 5 reached "any state enactment which altered the election law of a covered State in even a minor way,"[86] including, most controversially, changes from district to at-large elections. Mr. Justice John Harlan, dissenting, argued that section 5 should be read "to require federal approval only of those state laws that change either voter qualifications or the manner in which elections are conducted."[87] Asserting that "Congress did not attempt to restructure state governments,"[88] Harlan raised the basic issue whether the states should be left free to change their formulas for the drawing of district lines and the use or not of multimember districts. Despite the majority's conclusion that Congress did indeed intend this federal supervisory presence, and that it was a permissible exercise of power, later cases leave the issue in doubt.

In *Perkins* v. *Matthews*, the majority in effect reaffirmed the *Allen* ruling, holding that federal approval was necessary for (1) changed locations of polling places, (2) changed boundary lines through annexation, and (3) a changed method of electing aldermen from election by wards to an at-large election. Mr. Justice Harlan again dis-

---

84. Justices John Harlan and Potter Stewart dissented, believing the Court had "confused the issue of how much enforcement power Congress possesses under section 5 with the distinct issue of what questions are appropriate for congressional determination and what questions are essentially judicial in nature." 384 U.S. at 666 (Harlan, J., dissenting).

85. 393 U.S. 544 (1969). See also *Hadnott* v. *Amos*, 394 U.S. 358 (1969).

86. 393 U.S. at 566.
87. Id. at 591 (Harlan, J., concurring and dissenting).
88. Id. at 585.

agreed with the requirement for federal approval as to the changed boundary lines and the at-large election, and Mr. Justice Black dissented in all respects, as he had in *Allen*.[89] Chief Justice Warren Burger concurred, Mr. Justice Harry Blackmun concurred, "[g]iven the decision in *Allen* . . . ,"[90] which had been decided before either was a member of the Court. Their apparent doubts crystallized in *Holt* v. *Richmond* in 1972—by now joined also by Mr. Justice William Rehnquist—in which they expressed their willingness in an "appropriate case" to "reconsider the holding in *Allen* and *Perkins*."[91]

89. 400 U.S. at 397, 401.
90. Id. at 397.
91. *Holt* v. *Richmond*, 406 U.S. 903 (1972). Justices Byron White and Lewis Powell did not participate, suggesting the possibility of a majority willing to reconsider *Allen* and *Perkins*.
Georgia v. *United States*, 351 F. Supp. 444 (N.D. Ga.), probable jurisdiction noted, — U.S. — (1972), a case argued before the Supreme Court on February 21–22, 1973, raises these issues. The issue was whether the Georgia 1972 reapportionment act, which changed the boundaries of nearly all election districts within the state, was covered by section 5 of the Voting Rights Act of 1965. The claim of coverage was based on *Allen* and *Perkins* as well as the assertion that the redistricting, including changes in multimember and single-member districting arrangements, had the effect of diluting the voting strength of Negro voters. See Brief Amici Curiae for NAACP et al., *Georgia* v. *United States*, No. 72–75 (Oct. 1972 Term, U.S. Sup. Ct.).
NAACP v. *New York*, — F. Supp. — (D. D.C.), probable jurisdiction noted, — U.S. — (1972), argued before the Supreme Court on February 27–28, 1973, raises other issues under the 1965 Act. In this case the State of New York sued to obtain exemption for three counties in New York that had been brought within the coverage of sections 4 and 5 of the 1965 Act by the 1970 Amendments Act. The specific question before the Court, when the United States declined to defend the action, was whether the NAACP could intervene to do so. See Brief for Appellants, *NAACP* v. *New York*, No. 72–129 (Oct. Term 1972, U.S. Sup. Ct.).

Despite the apparent doubts of some members of the Court as to the validity of a requirement for federal approval of changes in voting qualifications and procedures by the states, the Court continued to find literacy tests suspect. *Gaston County* v. *United States*[92] involved an application to reinstate a literacy test previously suspended under the automatic suspension provision. With only Mr. Justice Black dissenting, the majority held that it was proper to consider whether such a literacy test would be racially discriminatory in light of the long pattern of separate and inferior schools for black residents now of voting age. Mr. Justice Harlan concluded that even "'Impartial' administration of the literacy test today would serve only to perpetuate these inequities in a different form."[93]

Racially discriminatory restrictions on the right to vote come in many packages, some blatantly direct and others beguilingly wrapped in the paraphernalia of apparently routine aspects of the political process. As already noted, the most outrageous interferences with the franchise have sometimes fallen as a result of judicial action grounded squarely on the prohibitions of the Fifteenth Amendment. More often, legislative assistance is needed, of which the most important has been the Voting Rights Act of 1965. Its most important weapon—once literacy tests had been eliminated by the 1965 and 1970 legislation—was the provision in section 5 requiring federal approval of proposed changes in voting qualifications and voting procedures. By the spring of 1973 there had been more than 2,500 submissions under section 5. The nearly 150 objections by the attorney general were responsible for protecting

92. 395 U.S. 285 (1969).
93. Id. at 297.

voters against discriminatory changes without litigation.[94] The first judicial review of an objection by the attorney general resulted in Supreme Court endorsement of his objection in a *per curiam* affirmance of a three-judge federal district court judgment in *Petersburg* v. *United States*.[95] The case involved a proposed annexation by the City of Petersburg of areas that would have increased the white population of the city by nearly half, while eliminating the black majority. When the city submitted its annexation proposal to the attorney general, as required by section 5 and *Perkins* v. *Matthews, supra,* the attorney general, acting through the assistant attorney general, civil rights division, objected. The ground was dilution of the black voting proportion, particularly in view of at-large elections for city councilmen. In combination, these provisions had a discriminatory effect on voting. The city's suit in challenge of that ruling was rejected by the district court. Although that court found a legitimate governmental purpose for the annexation, it concluded that the city did not sustain the "heavy burden for a community in a state with Virginia's history of past racial discrimination" of proving that the change "would not have the *effect* of discriminatorily depriving Negroes of the franchise on account of race or color."[96]

Conclusion

The Fourteenth and Fifteenth Amendments to the Constitution of the United States provide the basis for a considerable judicial role in protecting against interferences with the right to vote.

94. The Lawyers' Committee for Civil Rights Under Law, Report no. 10 (March 1973).
95. — U.S. — (1973), affirming — F. Supp. — (D.D.C. 1972).
96. — F. Supp. at —.

For many decades after the adoption of these two amendments, however, the courts were more inclined to rhetoric about democratic values than judicial protection of the franchise, even when assisted by moderately strong congressional action. With more recent recognition by the Supreme Court of the United States that the franchise cannot be limited except for a compelling state interest,[97] there no longer should be any doubt about the willingness of the courts to use prohibitions in the Fourteenth and Fifteenth Amendments to forbid restrictions on the right to vote that have a racially discriminatory purpose or effect.[98]

When Congress has acted pursuant to its enforcement powers under these amendments and pursuant to its revisory power over state voting laws in article I, section 4, the Supreme Court has been generally willing to endorse legislative proposals to deal with covert as well as overt discrimination. Even here uncertainties remain. As already noted, the crucially important decisions in *Allen* and *Perkins*, without which sec-

97. *Dunn* v. *Blumstein*, 405 U.S. 330 (1972). See also *Reynolds* v. *Simms*, 377 U.S. 533, 562 (1964); *Carrington* v. *Rash*, 380 U.S. 89, 93–94 (1965); *Harper* v. *Virginia State Board of Elections*, 383 U.S. 663, 667 (1966); *Cipriano* v. *City of Houma*, 395 U.S. 701, 706 (1969); *Kramer* v. *Union Free School District No. 15*, 395 U.S. 621, 626–25 (1969); *Evans* v. *Corman*, 398 U.S. 419, 421–22 (1970).
98. One exception, beyond the range of this discussion, is the apparent unwillingness of the Supreme Court to limit the gerrymander, frequently employed as a device for racially discriminatory legislative districting. Although the Court is ostensibly willing to strike down racially motivated districting plans [*Gomillion* v. *Lightfoot*, 364 U.S. 339 (1960); *Fortson* v. *Dorsey*, 379 U.S. 437 (1965)], the Court demands a burden of proof that seems impossible to meet [*Wright* v. *Rockefeller*, 376 U.S. 52 (1964); *Whitcomb* v. *Chavis*, 403 U.S. 124 (1971); *Mahon* v. *Howell*, — U.S. — (1973)].

tion 5 of the Voting Rights Act of 1965 would lose much of its force, are under attack.[99] Moreover, efforts to end discriminatory restrictions on the franchise, by court and by legislature, tell only part of the story. Even where there are no racially motivated restrictions on access to the ballot, problems of securing increased voter participation remain discouragingly difficult. Voter participation is much lower in the United States than other Western countries, especially among black citizens, North as well as South. It is ironic that efforts to dismantle discriminatory devices in the South have been somewhat more successful than efforts to encourage voter participation in areas where discrimination is absent.[100] Efforts to secure broader participation in elections for community school boards and neighborhood planning boards, for example, have not been notably successful, particularly in urban areas.[101]

Efforts to eliminate discrimination and to broaden the franchise must not be relaxed because of apparent success in the courts and in legislative bodies. Victories there will be transitory, unless the will for broadened exercise of the fundamental prerogative of a democratic society is implanted deep in the hearts and minds of citizens.

99. See notes 89-91 above.

100. In mounting a renewed drive for voter registration outside the South, Vernon Jordan, executive director of the National Urban League, concludes that the right to vote is still "abridged by a web of antiquated regulations that discriminate against the black and the poor, a web that affects the entire country." Vernon Jordan, "Barriers to Black Political Participation," *Civil Rights Digest*, (October 1972), p. 2.

101. See, for example, Lewis Kaden and Michael Schwartz, "Election of Community Boards" (unpublished manuscript, 1972).

ON POLITICS, BLACKS, AND THE WORLD, FRANKLY SPEAKING

By Henry A. Bryant

TABLE OF CONTENTS

	Page
I AN OVERVIEW SINCE "54"	33

The Black Revolution or the Awakening of the American Social Conscience	33
The Revolutionary Phase	34
Presidential Politics and Blacks	35
Grass Roots Response	36
Ideological Response	37
Rightist Politicians -- The Prophets of Doom	38
The New Reconstruction	39
Results and Meaning	39

II WHAT MUST BE DONE	40

Organization	40
State and National Conventions	41
A Black Political Party	41
Peculiar Political Position of American Blacks	41
Ideological Preparation -- An Illustration of its Importance	42

III A WORLD VIEW	43

Pan-Africanism	43
The OAU and Blacks	44
Towards an International African Peoples Congress	45

ON POLITICS, BLACKS, AND THE WORLD, FRANKLY SPEAKING

By Henry A. Bryant

I AN OVERVIEW SINCE "54"

Politics in America since 1954 has shown some remarkable "changes" both good and bad, but mostly bad. In 1954, the Brown Decision was passed abolishing the Plessey Decision of 1896, which had made it clear that Blacks would have to take it like Whites gave it to them on a separate basis, but with equal facilities. Now equality and fair play have never been American virtues of repute, especially where Blacks were concerned. Equal facilities? Just what is that? Blacks have matriculated in everything from inferior outhouses to horse troughs called drinking fountains. It was never intended for Blacks to have equal facilities, and the decision in 1954 overturning the Plessey Decision became a staging ground for hate campaigns, White citizens' councils, and costume balls in the honor of the Ku Klux Klan.

After 56 years of "keeping the nigger in his place," wherever that is, one Supreme Court decision issued by this tribunal said that it was all a mistake. This just wasn't the right ending to the fairy tale. The Redneck in "Hoosick Hollow," Mississippi, didn't even know what a Supreme Court was, and the decision certainly wasn't going to have any effect upon an accepted institution -- namely racism.

The Black Revolution or the Awakening of the American Sacred Conscience

It was to take men like Martin Luther King, who was to make an original and sincere attempt to bridge the chasm of racism, provincialism, and Anti-Blackism with a combination of peace -- Ghandian philosophy and methodology. The forces of peace and "soul force" were pitted against the beastly weapons of treachery, institutionalized racism, government corruption, corporate collusion, Black apathy, frustration, and carnivorous legal officials. This was a much more formidable foe than ever faced in the annals of mankind, even when his existence was primeval and he contested daily for survival with the most predatory and rapacious giant beasts of pre-history. However, undaunted he entered this jungle.

His methodology and philosophy rallied thousands to his aid with what might have been the last chance for the American conscience to redeem itself, and return to some semblance of humanity. It awakened the last vestiges of an almost dead American psyche which resulted in sit-ins, pray-ins, lay-ins; in short, the "ins" were in to stay for awhile. There were freedom rides based on the same philosophy and methodology, marches, and protest rallies. Could this be the true America? People wondered whether this could be the same America that robbed the Indian of his homeland, the African of his birthright, and the Mexican of his heritage.

The adrenalin in the Black body, mind, and soul began to pound. Maybe there was hope for the country. Could the meaning of the Declaration of Independence and the Constitution become a reality, in that "all men are created equal and endowed by their creator with certain inalienable rights?" The Human Rights movement steamrolled, and it appeared that after four hundred plus years of oppression and bloodshed, its time had come. It was to elect Presidents and change the course of American history -- for a while at least.

The Revolutionary Phase

Other phases of the total "Human Rights" movement came of age. Black males and females began to clamor for complete change, and to look for a vehicle and platform to channel that change. Some found it in the Student Movements from Sproul Hall at Berkeley to Cornell University. From these movements emerged young Black leaders and intellectuals. Men like Stokely Carmichael, Harry Edwards, Omari Musa, and Julian Bond became names in the news. Names outside of the college scene like H. Rap Brown, Eldridge Cleaver, and Bobby Seale, to name a few, raised the Nationalism of Blacks to a whole new peak of hope.

Para-political and political organizations such as the Black Panther Party with such articulate spokesmen as Huey P. Newton sprang up around the country. C.O.R.E. and S.N.C.C. became important organizations to channel protest. There were White youths working with Black youths, and it appeared that America now had a chance. It could be saved; it could be helped! It wasn't the mindless, capitalistic, profit-insane monster, awed and feared by the world after all -- or was it?

Presidential Politics and Blacks

Mr. John F. Kennedy, a name hardly known by Blacks prior to 1960, emerged as "the darling" of the 1960 election. Mr. Nixon tried and true, to the Establishment, that is, appeared a sure winner. Blacks who had endorsed Eisenhower, apparently saw his "standard bearer" Nixon as a likely choice. Nixon's ineptness in regard to knowing Blacks was nothing short of amazing. He committed tactical error after error. Although few Blacks knew of Nixon's apparent laxity as head of Eisenhower's "civil rights" program, few knew of his shocking anti-civil rights posture. Nixon appeared not to know that Blacks had been frustrated politically to the point that any "legitimate" gesture in their behalf would bring some type of immediate positive response. Kennedy found it with the King incident when he wrote Mr. King a "warm" telegram while he was in jail. Nixon did nothing. The response was overwhelming. Nixon's Black majority base disappeared overnight. He was not to forgive, nor soon forget.

Mr. Kennedy immediately presented no Civil Rights posture. His particular vernacular appeared to be "wait and see; don't go too fast." He was soon shaken out of his stupor by the events of the day. The murder of Medgar Evers at the hands of a deranged madman shook America. It demanded a response. A response that Mr. Kennedy could not avoid. So he responded, because he had no other choice. The next event came with the bombing of a "strong faction" of Black Revolutionaries -- a church -- by "Brave Sons of Liberty." Their enemy -- four young Black children, little girls at that. America was "outraged," well, at least they demanded a response. Kennedy was left with no choice again, and again he responded favorably, at least to the Movement. When the smoke cleared, Mr. Kennedy emerged as a national hero, a role which he relished. He went on to test the resistance of two Southern demagogues, segregationist Barnett of Mississippi, and the "simple little idiot" from Alabama, George Wallace. He couldn't go back now. Not only did he enter the Movement, but he co-opted it. Why not, he couldn't be President again without it. This mushroomed into his Civil Rights proposals on housing, public accommodations, and the amendments to destroy the Poll Tax. It was more than fate that ended it all in November of 1963. Blacks were sad! Their Messiah was dead. The obituary contained all the points mentioned above. However, it contained nothing on his assassination program, nor his beginning of the surveillance (bugging) program against Black groups, which was implemented by his brother, Robert. Well, so much for that!

The Johnson program was an instant replay, in that it was left to him to implement the Kennedy program. He couldn't afford to go back, it would have meant political suicide. Barry Goldwater, could he really be that stupid? Was he for real? This certainly was no period for a reactionary conservative.

In the middle of it all, the Viet Nam War leaped into headlines. Blacks, poor Whites, and Chicanos packed their bags and headed off to fight -- who was that they told us to fight? Oh yeah, the "Viet Cong or Cong" or something. The Department of Defense, or should it be called the War Department, because it appears that all they defend is corporate wealth, decided they were not going to let the Vietnamese decide for themselves, whatever the outcome, the type of government and economic structure they wanted. They just had to have a "Democracy," which has never worked in America, but you little Vietnamese people must have a Democracy -- period. Martin Luther King made the mistake, or was it a mistake, to speak out against justice everywhere, of speaking out against the war. Such is the stuff that makes widows. Mrs. King was alone now. Black America and the world mourned the death of a legitimate human being of international repute. It was for sure a rarity in America.

Grass Roots Response

Blacks between the years of 1964-68 took to the streets. It was spontaneity which would have amazed even Frantz Fanon. Not only was there now a deer season, duck season, bear season, and quail season, there was now a "riot season," or more clearly, a "nigger season." The response was brutality and some small concessions. Brutality like Bull Connors. The memory of hoses, dogs, bombing, vermin, and invective-strewn policemen, bent on maiming or killing -- us. The memory of death, tears, and Southern mobs.

Ideological Response

Ideologically, the stand for Black Nationalism brought one of the most articulate and brilliant leaders of any time, Malcolm X, who preached the concept of Blacks uniting worldwide and forming a Black Movement for change in the world everywhere. Black control of Black everything dealing with Black people everywhere that people are Black. It was to be social, economic, political, and cultural. Economic with businesses and industry in the Black community. Social in that Blacks realized their true worth as people. They demanded better education, knowledge of their own history and contributions. Political in that Blacks wanted the vote, organization, greater political representation, and control of the politicians who represented them in their community. Cultural in that Black Art, artists, films, movies, and Black Pride become essentials.

Stokely Carmichael and Rap Brown preached the ideology of Black power, which tended to be more localized than Black Nationalism. It purported the same basic control of all facets of the Black Community and was, in essence, the implementation of Black Nationalism.

However, the fears of the past were going to be visited on the present. By the end of the 1960's came the cry that "niggers were getting too much at the expense of White people." Style-conscious White politicians found that Civil and Human Rights were going out of style. It was time to get back into the old conservative suits. They were hanging, clean and pressed, in the closet.

The attack appeared to be multi-faceted. The police, the FBI, and the CIA would work together in a "reign of terror" against revolutionary groups. Mr. FBI himself and his henchmen would work with local police to smash the most infamous menace (according to the FBI) to American society -- the Black Panthers. It began in Chicago with Fred Hampton and Mark Clarke. "Brave and loyal to the cause" police officers opened fire on the Black Panther Party headquarters where two "dangerous criminals" in full battle array (bedsheets) waited to take the lives of policemen. They were in the most strategic revolutionary battle positions ever invented -- in their sleep. Needless to say, these two "dangerous" criminals attacked policemen with a wiltering rapid fire barrage of heavy "snores." However, undaunted Field Marshall Hanrahan and his troops braved these heavy "snores" and inflicted mortal wounds on their "dangerously" prostrate enemies.

This scene was to repeat itself all over the U.S. from Los Angeles to Oakland to Seattle. The plan appeared to be to kill or jail as many revolutionaries as possible. If they are dead, or while they are in jail, they can't organize. This certainly served notice to Blacks and men of goodwill everywhere, that the experiment in humanity was over. It would be business as usual.

Men were not the only victims. Classic beauties fell prey to the Stormtrooper brigades. Angela Davis is an unique example. The Marin shootout situation was in no way connected with Angela Davis, but American justice had thrown away her blindfold a long time ago. Its scales were too full of corrupted gold and greed to weigh anything legitimately. The balance had been tampered with too many times. The point in question was to try your revolutionaries in court, who cared whether an actual case existed against them? Even if you didn't convict them, you could effectively scare them off. Who would want to face the agony of the American Justice machine? It would also serve notice to other revolutionaries, dissidents, and poor people that even if we don't convict you, we will spend millions of the American taxpayers' money to try you with a traditionally conservative, all White, "model citizen" jury. If not, then when we release you, you'll think about it before you even conceive of trying to force any type of change. Joanne Little would fall victim to the same syndrome.

Rightist Politicians -- The Prophets of Doom

The last and probably the most brutal tactic was to pry apart any type of cohesion or coalition which might have developed between common people of every hue, through that tried and true American institution -- demographic racism. Why not? Hadn't it worked in the 1890's when the agrarian alliances between White farmers and Black farmers existed in the South? Hadn't it forced the failure of populism a generation ago? Yes, and it would work now.

The prophets of the "new" right or the new conservatism, were none other than the old politicians and patricians of racism. Their prophecy seemed to say: "Thus saith the prophets of the Right, there'll be no more -- no more programs designed to help poor people and minorities, no more jobs, no more change, no more money for education, and especially, no more niggers." However, the prophecy in terms of the "mores" tended to be, "Ye saith us, there shall be more -- more policemen, more firearms for the cops, more SWAT teams, more law and order, more M-16's for the Army, more bombing of Viet Nam, more money for the defense budget, more profits in the pockets of the businessmen and corporations at the expense of the common, everyday man, more bugging, more CIA violation of individual liberties, more B-52's . . ." The list appears eternal.

The New Reconstruction

The old fear of "nigger domination" was revitalized. It worked all over again. The election of Richard Nixon put into practice the ideology of the new Right. Human Rights projects were cut back remarkably. Officials were dismissed, and the Federal Laws in relationship to this were not enforced. Child care facilities were deleted altogether from the budget, and money for minority education was immediately attacked in the name of "Economic Efficiency." Nixon's Administration tended to give the red light to the dominant racists beneath the surface to once again emerge from their lairs of relative inactivity beneath the caverns of indifference to feed conspicuously and arrogantly on their favorite prey -- Black America.

Results and Meaning

The results were some dead, and many wounded, but nothing completely destroyed. Malcolm X, Martin L. King, Jonathan Jackson, George Jackson, and Medgar Evers, et al., paid the total price of death for their beliefs and struggles. There were many imprisoned and freed -- Angela Davis, Joanne Little, Bobby Seale, the San Quentin Six, Fleeta Drumgo, and Willie Tate. The list appears endless. It also meant exile. Exile for Eldridge Cleaver, Huey P. Newton (also tried), Stokely Carmichael, and others. Nevertheless, the struggle goes on. Every battle must have its R and R, but soldiers soon return

to the battle. The major contribution of the whole
movement was the level of consciousness that it gave
to the Black Community. Many Blacks ran for and won
elective offices bringing in Black mayors, etc. However, this means that a start has been made, but it certainly does not mean that this is the total answer.
There were Black mayors and such in the first Reconstruction; we need not say what happened. As sophistication grows among Blacks, sophistication also grows
among the Establishment. This means that Blacks must
develop a constantly higher sophistication. Blacks
have become much more aware of "tricks" and events used
by the Establishment to offset any Black gains.

II WHAT MUST BE DONE?

Lenin asked the same question over a generation ago.
It was important then, and it is important now. These
suggestions are basically those of the author, but they
are based on a sound political analysis.

Organization

Nothing, anywhere, at any time, before now, or after
now, will anything be done without sound preparation and
organization. Organization must be grassroots and community based. Vehicles to house the structure of such
an organization must be developed either as a para-political organization such as the Niagara Movement and other
Black movements before and in the early part of the century. This vehicle will serve as a "command post"
structure to aid Blacks in having a definitive place to
funnel their political activity. Whatever the organization, it must be funded directly by Blacks; no White
money should be accepted, except where there is <u>absolutely
no strings attached</u>. At no time should the organization
become dependent on White money or outside funds.

This community structure should be developed in each
individual Black community by people living in that community. This will prevent enclaves of power "to develop,"
and also prevent the total organization from being destroyed if one segment is infiltrated. Each organization
shall reflect the needs of each individual community. For
example, a welfare community should exhibit a welfare
rights stance. County-wide caucuses should be held where

all the people participate. There should be no prior
agenda where these meetings are concerned. This will
eliminate the structuring and domination by one essential group. People with similar political needs would
be allowed to form central committees and structure
their own strategy for solving the problem. When the
total caucus convened into a grand caucus, a position
paper should be written with the strategy of each group
stressed in detail. Each individual committee would
then aid each other in solving their problems in terms
of strategy, goals, and organization.

State and National Conventions

A State Convention should be held each year and the
same procedure followed, after sufficient strength has
been recognized, in planning a National Convention.
Essentially, the original grassroots foundation structure is followed right through to the National Convention.

A Black Political Party

The clamor for a Black Political Party rings louder
each day. The traditional Democratic and Republican
Parties are too well entrenched, too bureaucratic, too
White-oriented and liberal-dominated. The Death Knell
has surely sounded for these two parties. They can't
even serve the needs of poor Whites, let alone Blacks.
The Star of Exodus shines brighter for a trend towards
re-politicization. A new politics has been perceived.
No longer can Blacks simply ignore the fact that the
Republican Party is a party for people like Nixon. They
can no longer ignore the fact that men like Eastland and
Stennis have no business in the same political party with
Blacks. These men are Democrats. Many fear a third
party because of "no possible way to win syndrome,"
which has little validity because we certainly aren't
winning with the Democratic Party or the Republican Party.
These are facts which can't be denied. Most Black leaders oppose a Black Party because they fear the departure
of their own power. The basis of the Black political
party would be based on the strength of the organizations
discussed prior. It could not be successful unless it is.

Peculiar Political Position of American Blacks

Blacks in America are not in the political position
of Blacks everywhere else. Under colonialism in Africa,

the White man came there. He was never in the majority. In the Caribbean, both Blacks and Whites came. The White man never being in the majority there either. In the U.S. Blacks constitute a minority; in the rest of the world, they constitute a majority. As these nations clamor for independence, they can consequently place their nationalism into effect, even to the point of armed rebellion. In America, the solution to Black politics must be tied into a world Black movement. The struggle here is intensified many times over.

Ideological Preparation -- An Illustration of its Importance

Political Education classes are a must, and can be held everywhere. In basements, garages, or any openly accessible place. Probably the greatest political asset, and the intricate and unique mechanism known to mankind is that of the Human body. The mind is the focal point and guiding center of the mechanism. The Western Nations, especially the Americans, appear to have forgotten this, and the Third World people have been mainly victorious because they have not. Vastly destructive weaponry and technology are only initially useful against the Human body, but in an extended campaign, destroyed by it. With an ever-increasing technology, there occurs a lessening of dependence upon human faculties. There occurs a blight or pauperization of moral and human qualities, and the "will" or the "spirit" of the people lessens proportionally. The Western "Super Powers" rely basically on the superiority of their weaponry. This leads to an "ideological bankruptcy" which the entire west now suffers from. Their soldiers are given little ideological preparation. In short, they have no cause which can safely justify their presence in the crusade in which they are then engaged. The whole idea of making the "world safe for Democracy" has no validity being that the soldiers during the fighting are either Blacks, Chicano, or poor Whites. "Democracy" has very little real meaning to them. It cannot sustain their determined effort for longer than a year to 13 months. There are no more Alamos, no more Maines, and no more Pearl Harbors. The whole purpose of the campaign becomes circumspect. This circumspection in a long campaign increases to the point where only the soldier with the "will" sharpened considerably by strong and effective political indoctrination emerges as a vastly superior weapon to that of technology. The poor and Third World nations have it, because they have principally nothing else, and because it is a superior weapon, these peoples are increasingly victorious against the mammoth Western nations. It happened in Viet Nam with the Americans, in Algeria with the French, and in Angola with the Portuguese. It will continue to happen. Political indoctrination is a must.

III A WORLD VIEW

Pan-Africanism

The concept of total Nationalism for all Black people must be developed. The strength of the minority of Blacks in the U.S. will become increasingly more important with its ability to relate to the rise of Blacks everywhere. Since 1945, the independence of Third World nations have been greatly accelerated. This means that World Wars such as those which occurred in 1914 and 1939 are a thing of the past. In essence, these were the White Civil Wars. Latrop Stoddard wrote in 1920, "To me the Great War was the first of the White Civil Wars, which whatever its outcome, must gravely compromise the course of racial relations." (Stoddard, 1920). "World War I was over spheres of influence in Asia and colonies in Africa." (W.E.B. DuBois, 1946). Adolf Hitler wrote, "If I try to gauge my work, I must consider, first of all, that I've contributed in a world that had forgotten the notion, to the triumph of the idea of primacy of the Race." (Adolf Hitler, October 21, 1941).

No longer will the Third World peoples have to go to war if the White world chooses to fight itself. The colonies of Europe have disappeared. No longer will Algeria have to go to war with France. This undoubtedly has brought about, and continues to bring about, a polarization of the world in terms of race. This means that the next war must be a race war, because the whole idea of fighting a world war for the domination of colonial interest and spheres of influence along these lines are dead. It's a question of the Western world preparing itself for survival. Being that there are only two Western nations strong enough today to defend the entire West from the Third

World, mainly Russia and the U.S., the likelihood of them striking each other is remote. If it occurs, this will leave the Third World almost in a position of world domination faster than expected. It will eventually come anyway. Viet Nam and the reversal of the Western nations in recent wars illustrate that the job of preventing this cannot be done through military hardware alone. The intelligence communities of these nations will work hard at staging overthrows of foreign governments through co-option of leadership, assassination, unilateral trade pacts, economic conciliations, and the discrediting of foreign leadership in the Third World nations, who remain "hostile to the Western world." This can only stall the issue.

Let me reiterate that the next war, or the next series of wars, must be racial wars. This is because the Third World contains most of the world's resources. In the past, these people were under the domination of the Western world, therefore their resources were taken by the Western nations. This is why these nations fought each other to gain a bigger share of the colonial wealth in World War I and II, which as stated before, were White Civil Wars. The Third World was involved because they were subjects of the Western world. Today this no longer remains. If the Western nations want these resources, they will have to pay the price for them, thus slightly lowering their standards of living, take them in war, or set up puppet governments of neo-colonialism in these nations to allow Western businesses to reap the benefits of cheap labor and to give them continued access to the goods of these countries. Ultimately, this will fail, which will virtually lead to Armageddon.

The OAU and Blacks

The Organization of African Unity is a prime source of Black World organization. At this writing, certain Black nations boycotted the meeting. This type of non-cooperation must stop. These Black leaders who boycotted the meeting are either those who have been co-opted by White Western nations or those coming to the Western nations with their hands out, or those in the process of being co-opted. The Organization of African Unity is a prime forum for Black World reorganization, and the Western intelligence community knows that and will attempt to sabotage and subvert its purposes by any means at their disposal.

The possibility exists for the Black Caucus to apply for membership in the OAU. Absurd? Not so! Any means of cementing the relationships between Blacks in the world community should be examined and followed. There could be a dialogue to determine where Blacks in America and Africa would work together to further their own interest. The main reason why the author suggests the Black Caucus is that they as a national body could engender the publicity necessary to awaken the conscience of Blacks everywhere in the U.S.

Towards an International African Peoples Congress

A worldwide International African Peoples Congress could grow out of this, calling for conferences annually of African peoples and peoples of African descent everywhere. It could be a yearly repeat of the now-defunct but once successful Bandung Conference, which called for Third World peoples to unite everywhere. The African Peoples Congress could be similar to that; a worldwide annual Bandung Conference could be instituted where all Third World peoples would participate. With cooperation of all sections of the Black world, this is possible. It must be implemented, or in time it will spell the doom of the Black World, and ultimately of the Third World.

This has been Henry Bryant speaking frankly about politics, Blacks, and the World Political System. The remarks are those of the author solely. They are the result of years of studying, analyzing, and perceiving. They are the blessings of God's gifts to me, and it is my duty to use what he has given me.

Henry A. Bryant

Black People and the Tyranny of American Law

By Haywood Burns

ABSTRACT: The American legal system has not managed to escape the racism that permeates American life. Both historically and contemporaneously, the law has been the vehicle by which the generalized racism in the society has been made particular and converted in policies and standards of social control. Notwithstanding many countervailing experiences, many black Americans see their dominant experience with the law as that of the law's victim. Present efforts at using the law as an instrument of social change in order to relieve this victimization are encumbered by a lack of black direction of and control over the resources, policy, and personnel ostensibly organized to combat racism. The tyranny of a racist legal structure and the powerlessness of blacks in the face of white hegemony over most of the major legal institutions—public and private—which have been established to attempt to eradicate white racism, must both be answered by the reassertion by the black bar and the black community of their interests in shaping the decisions which so profoundly affect their lives. If leadership of this character articulates black priorities from the perspective of the community centrally affected, then all willing elements of the society can contribute usefully to the attainment of the goals of freedom with dignity for all.

Haywood Burns is National Director of the National Conference of Black Lawyers (NCBL). Educated at Harvard, Cambridge, and Yale Universities, he is the author of The Voices of Negro Protest in America *(Oxford, 1963), as well as numerous articles, book reviews, and poems. He is also an Adjunct Associate Professor of Law at New York University. Previously he served as a staff attorney with the NAACP Legal Defense and Educational Fund, Inc.; as law clerk to the Honorable Constance B. Motley, U.S. District Court; and as an Associate at the New York law firm of Paul, Weiss, Rifkind, Wharton and Garrison.*

IN classical theories of democracy, the laws are supposed to reflect "the will of the people"—or at least of the majority. From the point of view of black people in this country, American law has been all too successful in this regard; for, in a country permeated by white racism,[1] the legal system has been and continues to be racist in character. More than a century ago, in analyzing democracy in America, Alexis de Tocqueville warned of the "tyranny of the majority," pointing out that in the absence of safeguards for the protection of minority rights, American democracy becomes just another form of tyranny.[2] Tocqueville might have gone further and pointed out that in a majority racist society what obtains these circumstances is a racist tyranny over the racial minority. For American blacks, too often the safeguards either do not exist, or are not applied. Too often blacks have known the law only as a sword, and not as a shield.

There have, of course, been myriad countervailing experiences with the law, where it has been used as an instrument of constructive social change to the benefit of blacks—more so in the most recent past than throughout our history.[3] However, the dominant experience has been one in which the law acted as the vehicle by which the generalized racism in the society was made particular and converted into standards and policies of subjugation and social control. Most white Americans tend to view the historic role of the law in this country as that of a tool for the expansion of liberty, and they are largely correct as to themselves—especially if they are not poor (which most are not). However, etched deep in the collective consciousness of American blacks is the role that the law has played in their oppression. It is a present perception which comports with both the historical and contemporary reality.

THE PAST

Slavery

The institution of American chattel slavery is unique in the experience of human kind—unique in its brutality, unique in its drive to degrade and depersonalize those persons enslaved.[4] The American slave system relied heavily upon the American legal system for the creation and the perpetuation of the institution of American chattel slavery. This is not to say that the law itself was responsible for bringing slavery into existence. It was, to a large extent, recognizing as de jure a de facto situation that had been developing for some time. What is true, though, is that the law played a critical role in the institutionalization of American slavery, defining, sanctioning, and ossifying it, and protecting its presence upon the American landscape for centuries.

It is not often recalled that in the early seventeenth century, during the days of the first settlements in this country, there was at first no clearly defined status of "slave." White Europeans and black Africans existed side by side in various stages of unfreedom. Some form of bondage was a very common experience, and there was considerable confusion over and imprecision about the use of the term "slave." It certainly was not synonymous and inter-

---

1. See *Report of the National Advisory Commission on Civil Disorders* (New York: Bantam, 1968), p. 10.
2. Alexis de Tocqueville, *Democracy in America* (1841; reprint ed., New York: Vintage, 1945), p. 269.
3. See William H. Hastie, "Toward an Equalitarian Legal Order: 1930-1950," THE ANNALS (May 1973), pp. 18-31.
4. See Kenneth M. Stampp, *The Peculiar Institution: Slavery in the Ante-Bellum South* (New York: Random House, 1956).

changeable with the word "Negro"—as it later grew to be. Black persons sometimes served a term of years and were then to be released from service and even in some instances to own or hold other blacks in servitude.[5]

Increasingly, however, throughout the seventeenth century the situations of the blacks in bondage and the whites in bondage diverged: the plight of the white steadily improved and that of the black became more debased. It was the law that was responsible for the crucial developments in this whole process, which by century's end had defined the perimeters of a slave system and had permanently locked the black, by reason of his blackness, on the inside. This was accomplished by white men who, sitting in Colonial legislatures, passed laws making bondage for *blacks* (1) a lifetime condition and (2) a hereditary condition.[6] Thus the law not only fastened onto the captive African for all of his days, but it marked as well the unborn, condemning not an individual or a generation, but an entire people to the night of slavery.

Nation-building

With a revolution for liberty and the birth of a new nation, the so-called founding fathers were presented with a prime opportunity to resolve in favor of freedom the contradictions of a nation which was established in the interest of liberty, yet everywhere kept men and women enslaved. After much debate, the opportunity was missed. Slavery was to be a part of the new America. Apparently, even the more progressive of the founding fathers, those with scruples against slavery, were unprepared to tamper with so much private property and unable to accept fully the notion of blacks being their equals.[7] Blacks were, at this point in time—as they would be many times thereafter—the victims of an American pragmatism that bartered and compromised their lives away in a process from which they had been totally excluded—sacrificed to the exigencies of certain white imperatives. Black school children of today must still look at the Constitution of 1789 and see enshrined in our fundamental law, the guaranteed continuation of the slave trade,[8] the required return of fugitive slaves,[9] and the counting of enslaved, disfranchised blacks as three-fifths persons for purposes of political representation.[10]

Pre–Civil War

It was the law, through the slave codes of the eighteenth and nineteenth centuries, which governed in oppressive detail the lives of millions of black slaves. The slave codes, by their terms, denied a legal personality to blacks, barring them from bringing law suits or testifying against a white person. Through elaborate statutory schemes, the slave codes regulated the movement of blacks, denied any family relationship, and applied criminal sanctions according to a different and harsher

5. See Winthrop D. Jordan, *White over Black* (Chapel Hill: University of North Carolina Press, 1968), p. 74; Paul C. Palmer, "Servant into Slave: The Evolution of the Legal Status of the Negro Laborer in Colonial Virginia," *South Atlantic Quarterly* 65 (1966), pp. 355-70.

6. See Jordan, *White over Black*, pp. 44-98; Assembly Proceedings, September 1664, Liber WH & L, 28-29, Maryland Archives, I, 533-34, as quoted in *Civil Rights and the American Negro*, Albert P. Blaustein and Robert L. Zangrando, eds. (New York: Trident, 1968), p. 9.

7. See Staughton Lynd, "Slavery and the Founding Fathers," in *Black History*, Melvin Drimmer, ed. (Garden City, N.Y.: Doubleday, 1968), pp. 115-31.

8. U.S. Constitution, article I, section 9.
9. U.S. Constitution, article IV, section 2.
10. U.S. Constitution, article I, section 2.

standard than applied to whites.¹¹ The law confirmed and guaranteed the debased situation of the slave, and the entire legal apparatus was ultimately reinforced by the Taney dictum, in the *Dred Scott* case, that the Negro "had no rights which the white man was bound to respect." ¹²

Neither was the oppressive role of the law in this period entirely a regional phenomenon. North of the Mason-Dixon line it was the law which relegated so-called free blacks to an inferior status, barring blacks from certain types of employment, banning them from within the borders of certain territories, requiring segregated schools, and withholding from blacks the franchise.¹³

Post–Civil War

A northern victory in the Civil War and the passage of the Thirteenth, Fourteenth, and Fifteenth Amendments were not sufficient to arrest this process completely; for immediately after the Civil War whites turned to the law once again hoping to duplicate in so far as was possible, the vertical white-black relationship that existed prior to emancipation. The wholesale passage of black codes was designed to keep blacks: close to the land, away from certain types of occupations, away from white women, and subservient.¹⁴ In fact, without an identifying date, it is often difficult to tell a post–Civil War black code from a pre–Civil War slave code.

After Reconstruction the law was once again a major white weapon for wrenching rights from the hands of blacks, destroying the many black gains that had been made during that period. It was the law which launched the strange career of Jim Crow, codifying the customs and usages of segregation and giving them universal application in the southern states.¹⁵ It was the law—aided by the extra-legal, though community sanctioned, force of lynch law—which disfranchised hundreds of thousands of blacks in the late nineteenth and early twentieth century, stripping from black people the hard won black political power. The grandfather clause, the literacy test, and the poll tax were all legal devices designed to block black people from the polls. It was in this period, as well, that an increasingly conservative Supreme Court cut back on the breadth of the Civil War Amendments, giving them an increasingly narrow interpretation to the detriment of black people, a trend that finally culminated in acceptance as the law

---

11. For cases and statutes in this area see William Goodell, *The American Slave Code* (1853; reprint ed., New York: New American Library, 1969); George M. Stroud, *A Sketch of the Laws Relating to Slavery in the Several States of the United States of America*, 2nd ed. (Philadelphia: Henry Longstreth, 1856); Helen Catterall, *Judicial Cases Concerning American Slavery and the Negro* (Washington, D.C.: Carnegie Institution of Washington, 1926–37). See also Pauli Murray, "Roots of the Racial Crisis: Prologue to Policy" (J.S.D. thesis, Yale University, 1965).

12. *Scott* v. *Sanford*, 60 U.S. (19 How.) 393 (1857).

13. See Leon Litwack, *North of Slavery* (Chicago: University of Chicago Press, 1961); *Roberts* v. *City of Boston*, 59 Mass. (Cush.) 198 (1849).

14. See, for example, An act to establish and regulate the domestic relations of persons of color, and to amend the law in relation to paupers and vagrancy, Acts of the General Assembly of the State of South Carolina, 1864–1865, pp. 291–304, quoted in Blaustein and Zangrando, *Civil Rights*, pp. 218–25; see also W. E. B. Dubois, *Black Reconstruction in America* (London: Cass and Co., 1964), pp. 196–97, 331, 351; John Hope Franklin, *From Slavery to Freedom, A History of Negro Americans*, 3rd ed. (New York: Random House, 1969), pp. 187–90, 303, 327.

15. See Blaustein and Zangrando, *Civil Rights*, pp. 283–88, 294–321; C. Vann Woodward, *The Strange Career of Jim Crow*, 2nd rev. ed. (New York: Oxford University Press, 1966), pp. 67–109.

of the land of the *Plessy* v. *Ferguson* "separate, but equal" pronouncement.[16] The citadel of legally established and sanctioned apartheid remained largely inviolate throughout most of the twentieth century, until the major legal assaults of the U.S. Supreme Court decision in *Brown* v. *Board of Education*[17] in 1954 and the Civil Rights Act of 1957[18]—the first federal civil rights legislation in the country since Congress had passed the Civil Rights Act of 1875.[19]

THE PRESENT

The numerous successful legal attacks upon segregation have not solved the problem of racism and the law for black people today. Racism is still part and parcel of the daily reality of the functioning of the justice system. Black lawyers, plaintiffs, defendants, and witnesses are still subjected to the overtly racist attitudes, actions, and comments of an overwhelmingly white justice system. Black people are likewise affronted by a legal system that so often works against them and too seldom works for them, when they have been victimized and the state should be under an obligation to prosecute the white perpetrators of the wrong.

At one point in our history the law reserved exclusively for white men the right to sit on juries.[20] Though jury statutes no longer state this exclusion, blacks are still systematically excluded from juries through unfair procedures for compiling prospective jury rolls and through racial use of the peremptory challenge by the prosecutor. As a result, legions of black men and women are continually having their liberty and property taken away and their lives put in jeopardy by juries from which their peers have been systematically excluded.[21]

In the nineteenth century there were legal provisions that prevented blacks from bringing law suits against whites, or from testifying when white interests were involved. Though this situation no longer legally obtains, it is the common experience of black litigants that judges and juries are often likely to outweigh the testimony of several black witnesses with the testimony of one white one; that in a personal injury case the leg or arm of a white litigant is valued more highly than that of a black one.[22]

In the past, in some statutes different penalties were set out for whites and blacks for the same offense. Though this is no longer the case, sentencing patterns, when taken as a whole, often reveal a significant disparity between sentences meted out to blacks and whites for the same offense.[23] One of the most egregious areas in this regard is in death sentences, in particular, death sentences for interracial sex crimes. Sexual mutilation was at one time the statutory penalty reserved almost exclusively for blacks and Indians for interracial sex crimes.[24] In modern times it seems to have been the death penalty. Since the 1930s, 455 persons have been executed for rape in this country. Four hundred five of these

16. 163 U.S. 537 (1896).
17. 347 U.S. 483 (1954).
18. 71 Stat. 634 (1957).
19. 18 Stat. 335 (1875).
20. See *Strauder* v. *West Virginia*, 100 U.S. 303 (1880).

21. See *Swain* v. *Alabama*, 380 U.S. 202 (1965); Charles Morgan, "Segregated Justice," in *Southern Justice*, Leon Freidman, ed. (New York: Pantheon, 1965); note, "Fair Jury Selection Procedures," *Yale Law Journal* 75 (1965), p. 322.
22. See Morgan, note 21 above, p. 157.
23. Marvin Wolfgang and Bernard Cohen, *Crime and Race: Conceptions and Misconceptions* (New York: Institute of Human Relations Press, 1970), p. 81.
24. Jordan, *White over Black*, p. 155.

persons have been black.[25] In other areas of law related to sentencing, where great amounts of discretion are involved—such as commutation of sentences—overall patterns of disparity of treatment can also be discerned.[26]

Quite apart from any direct or explicit considerations, the law, by reason of its structure—its procedural rules and substantive doctrines—operates to the disadvantage of the poor and minority person. This structural inequality brings about a type of institutional subordination [27] based on class and caste—class, because so much of this institutional unfairness is related to the amount of money a person has; caste, because such a vastly disproportionate number of the poor in this country are also members of the nation's racial minorities.

A prime example can be seen in the operation of the money bail system, which jails one group of citizens for weeks, months, and sometimes years before trial, while another group goes free. Both are equally presumed innocent; money is the only discriminating factor. As a result, the country's jails are packed to overflowing with the nation's poor—with red, brown, black, and yellow men and women showing up in greatly disproportionate numbers.[28]

These problems of institutional subordination along racial lines due to the law's structural inequality are not, however, limited to matters of criminal justice. There is structural inequality in the owner-biased landlord-tenant law [29] and creditor bias in the commercial law.[30] In administrative law as measured by the standard of due process required, there is often less respect and protection for the matters of concern to poor and minority citizens than that accorded major commercial and propertied interests.[31] Further, in the previous century black people were barred from certain states and territories by law. Today, large-acre zoning laws effectively put certain geographical areas off-limits to blacks.[32] In addition, the law continues to be used as a tool for depriving black people of effective political participation through the exercise of the franchise, for example, where "at-large" systems of voting can be used to assure that a black minority will never be in a position in the particular locale in question to elect a political representative of its own choosing.[33]

Political repression

Black people are, as well, increasingly victimized by the growing political uses

---

25. U.S. Department of Justice, National Prisoner Statistics: Capital Punishment, 1930–1968 (1969), p. 10.
26. Wolfgang and Cohen, *Crime and Race,* p. 85.
27. Institutional subordination is the placing or keeping of persons in a position or status of inferiority by means of attitudes, actions, or institutional structures which do not use color itself as the subordinating mechanism, but instead use other mechanisms indirectly related to color. This definition is derived from the U.S. Commission on Civil Rights study, "Racism in America and How to Combat It" (1970), p. 6.
28. See National Conference on Bail and Criminal Justice, "Bail in the United States" (1964); Caleb Foote, "The Coming Constitutional Crisis in Bail," *University of Pennsylvania Law Review* 113 (1965), p. 959.
29. See Emily Goodman, *The Tenant Survival Book* (Indianapolis: Bobbs-Merrill, 1972); Project on Social Welfare Law, Housing for the Poor, Rights and Remedies (New York: New York University School of Law, 1967).
30. See *The Law and the Low Income Consumer,* Carol Hecht Katz, ed. (New York: New York University School of Law, 1968).
31. See Charles Reich, "The New Property," *Yale Law Journal* 73 (1964), p. 733.
32. See John D. Johnston, Jr., "Land Use Control," *Annual Survey of American Law* 49 (1970).
33. See, for example, *Chavis* v. *Whitcomb,* 305 F. Supp. 1364 (S.D. Ind. 1969); *Petersburg* v. *U.S.,* — U.S. — (March 5, 1973).

of the law against the unpopular and the politically controversial, as the law is used for a tool of political repression in the service of racism, and in opposition to the legitimate aspirations of the black community for change. Political uses of the law certainly are not directed exclusively at black community activists, but since members of the black community make up such a large part of the cutting edge of the movement for social change in this country, the black community takes a large part of the brunt of the abuses of state power. Contemporary concern in the black community focuses upon the passage of new legislation that can be used as an instrument of repression; for example, preventive detention, "no-knock," and "stop and frisk" legislation, while not racially directed in its terms, is seen to pose a decided threat to the freedom of blacks. The Interstate Riot Act, or so-called Rap Brown Act,[34] which, in effect, makes certain thoughts criminal if one happens to be thinking them while crossing a state line, is a ready weapon to attack politically active black spokesmen. Legislation that limits grand jury immunity and, in effect, compels grand jury testimony upon pain of imprisonment, flies in the face of traditional notions concerning the privilege against self-incrimination.[35] It is part of a much larger phenomenon which supports governmental use of the grand jury process to suppress and inhibit political activism—a phenomenon of special moment to the black community at a time when it is attempting to coalesce and organize its efforts to secure change.

The fact that the U.S. Supreme Court apparently looks with favor upon such practices,[36] coupled with what is perceived as a more generalized trend in Supreme Court decisions toward the erosion of fundamental rights, is another source of distress for black people.

Wholly apart from statutes or appellate decisions, it is the day-to-day administration of the law—particularly, the criminal justice system—which shapes the attitudes of black people about the law. There is concern about the street-level abuse—verbal, psychological, and physical—attendant upon the enforcement of the law in black communities. The para-military aspect of law enforcement has taken on an even more decided emphasis in recent times with police resorting to some of the latest technological advances in equipment and weaponry, greatly aided by grants under the federal Law Enforcement Assistance Administration to patrol and control black communities. The harshness of the developments are exacerbated by the rampant police corruption and the selective enforcement of the law witnessed by minority persons in their communities.[37]

Of late, the violence of officialdom has gone beyond unprovoked police attacks upon the headquarters and offices of political activists or upon the persons of political activists as they come to court, to the murders at Kent State, Jackson State, South Carolina State (Orangeburg), Southern University, Attica, Chicago (Fred Hampton and Mark Clark), and elsewhere.

Police practices in dealing with black political spokesmen give black people further cause for pause and further support the view that the law continues to be an instrument of racism and repression where they are concerned. There

34. 18 U.S.C. 2101, 2102.
35. 18 U.S.C. 6002–6003.
36. See *Kastigar* v. *U.S.*, 406 U.S. 441 (1972).

37. See Paul Chevigny, *Police Power* (New York: Pantheon, 1969); Commission to Investigate Allegations of Police Corruption and the City's Anti-Corruption Procedures, *Commission Report 1972* (New York City's Knapp Commission).

is the questionable manner in which informants are being employed. All too often they are either unsound individuals, or persons with serious charges or possible long sentencing facing them, who are told to produce evidence under circumstances that invite entrapment. There is, as well, the use of the *agent provocateur*, the person who infiltrates political groups and instigates activity that may subject the members and leadership of the group to arrest and imprisonment. This unsavory police practice has been used against black political activists to the overall detriment of the image of the police and the law in the mind of much of black America.[38]

These practices must be seen against a backdrop of increased police surveillance of private citizens in many sectors of life—but especially political activity. The amassing of dossiers and keeping of data banks on persons quite unrelated to criminal activity has served both to anger and to chill those who seek to exercise First Amendment rights.

Electronic surveillance or "bugging," to the level of wholesale invasions of privacy and encroachments upon fundamental rights, is a source of deep concern for a people who for centuries had their lives constantly monitored and governed in minutest detail. In recent years the federal government had even gone so far as to maintain that it could conduct electronic surveillance in certain kinds of cases involving domestic security without first having to obtain judicial approval. The U.S. Supreme Court, however, was unanimous in its view that the government had no authority to contravene our fundamental liberties.[39]

Fear of the law as an instrument of repression on the part of a racial group that has experienced the law in this role is enhanced when the government blithely ignores constitutional safeguards to accomplish what it may view as a superior political purpose. The mass arrest of hundreds of persons during the Washington D.C., May Day activity without any semblance of "probable cause" raised just such a specter.

The money bail system is inequitable in its normal operation, making pretrial liberty depend on the size of a person's wallet. The inequity of the system is compounded in political cases, however, by the extremes to which the state goes in demanding exorbitant amounts of money as a condition of pretrial release. Often these amounts seem to bear no relationship to the likelihood of appearance at trial, but are, in fact, a species of political ransom.

The frequent charge of conspiracy in cases involving political activists is viewed as another example of political use of the law. Conspiracy has long been a charge to which the state would resort in attacking the controversial and/or politically disfavored defendant. The rules of evidence become much more elastic under such a charge, and no substantive crime need be proven. The amorphous nature of the law of conspiracy makes it a useful prosecutorial device. Angela Davis, Bobby Seale, Erika Huggins, the Panther Twenty-one, the Chicago Seven, the Harrisburg Eight: all were faced with conspiracy charges—though none was convicted.

A further difficulty with the law that faces blacks in modern times is the harassment of those who would plead their cause. Increasingly, lawyers—black and white—who have taken on

38. See Paul Chevigny, *Cops and Rebels* (New York: Pantheon, 1972).
39. *U.S.* v. *U.S. Dist. Court for the Eastern District of Michigan*, 407 U.S. 297 (1972).

the defense of black activists have themselves become the subject of official sanctions—facing contempt, bar discipline, or even criminal charges. This has happened to the degree that part of the struggle of black people with American law today is to protect their protectors.

The inequities and failings of the legal system, as far as black people are concerned, are capped by the barbarity and racism of a punishment system that is itself a crime. The warehousing of human beings that goes on in our nation's prisons is a well-documented national disgrace, which, once again, falls with disproportionate severity upon minority group prisoners—especially those who would organize in an effort to change their lot and end the crime of punishment.[40]

Thus, from the sidewalk to the big house, the ugly specter of legal racism still stalks today's American black man and woman.

Structure of the Profession

The law's racism—past and present—has been a substantial obstacle to black advance in this country. Despite this fact, the legal system still carries with it the possibilities of positive change in the direction of remedying many of the deprivations black people face in America. Offensive civil actions, criminal defense of activists working for change, and the test case all have their merit. As long as the law is regarded as only a component in a much larger change process, and not a panacea, it is evident that it is much too valuable a tool for black people to abandon at this point in time—if ever.

What is ironic, but perhaps not surprising, is that not only are black people afflicted by the legacy of a legal structure permeated with racism, but much of the structure of the institutional apparatuses that have grown up to attack this racism operates in ways inimical to black interests. At one point in time, black people played a major role in shaping and carrying out the legal strategies addressed to the problems of their own liberation. Under the guidance and direction of such legal giants as Charles Houston, William Hastie, Thurgood Marshall, James Nabrit, Jr., and others, and with the intellectual support of the Howard Law School, great civil rights advances through the law were plotted and carried out.[41] However, the situation of black leadership in the legal arena in the definition and solution of the major problems of black society in white America no longer obtains.

Of course, racism is a problem that affects all who live in America—black or white. All have a stake in its eradication—including those of its beneficiaries who would hate to see it go. However, to say that all are victimized by racism is not to say that all are victimized by it equally or in the same way. Blacks, as the chief direct victims, should have a critical say in the way in which their victimizers and victimization are to be addressed. In the presence of the villainous white racism, fair-minded persons should respect black people sufficiently to permit them to define their problems and lead in shaping the solutions. This is a crucial aspect of black's empowerment, self-determination, and decolonization. It is, as well, rightfully a part of white people's liberation—liberation from paternalism, from patronizing, from dictating to blacks what black problems

---

40. See Karl Menninger, *The Crime of Punishment* (New York: Viking, 1968); *Black Law Journal* 1, no. 2 (Summer 1971).

41. See Robert L. Carter, "The Black Lawyer," *Humanist* (September-October 1969), pp. 12, 13.

are and how they are to be solved. It is not an excuse for white abdication of responsibility or inaction in these areas. In the past, great contributions by lawyers of all races have been made to the legal struggle against racism. History has seen to it that there are very few black lawyers at the bar.[42] A major portion of the legal assault upon racism has been and will continue to be carried on by white attorneys—which is entirely appropriate, since white racism is all our problem. Close cooperation and close working relationships between the white and black bar in these areas certainly are indicated. However, representatives of the white bar need to relinquish their hold on the claim to control and direct black people's destinies, and be prepared to accept black leadership on matters of social policy where black people are primarily affected.

Today, most of the major decisions concerning legal strategies designed to address the issues having widest impact upon black America are made in institutions—private and public—that are not under black direction or control and which lack sufficient black input from either the black bar or the black community. The major financing of legal efforts on issues of critical importance to the black community goes to these institutions, for, despite the burgeoning efforts of black people at organization and self-help and the ever increasing number of well-credentialed blacks interested in applying legal skills in the service of their communities, foundations and other philanthropic sources continue to fund in their own image.

The result of this set of circumstances is that choices are made of the greatest moment to the black community—concerning what issues are important, what is their priority, what political activists are worthy of defense, what political activists are not, where will the millions of dollars of private and public funds be allocated, and so forth—without the assistance of the legally trained persons from the community most affected, or without the ability of members of those communities to exercise much control over these decisions which so deeply affect their lives.

One of the most serious, if not the ultimate, of indignities is the tyranny of those who control the gathering and dissemination of the written and spoken word concerning the black situation. Even there the majority group would have black people submit themselves to the will and the power of those non-blacks who control. For example, not only are black people disadvantaged by a white racist legal structure and hindered in their efforts to correct this situation by a white-dominated civil rights legal establishment, but the interpretation of their situation is given over to persons from outside the group centrally involved. They cannot tell their own story without having it screened through white interpreters. This is not to negate the right of white writers and editors to write and prepare publications on blacks; nor is it to disparage personally the white individuals, often persons of great ability, who follow this course. It is only to say that in the 1970s, in the presence of so many fine, trained, and talented black legal personages equipped by training and sensitivity to address and interpret the black situation, it is a great affront to the black bar and the black community, and the product of the grossest racial myopia, when those responsible for gen-

---

42. Though black people make up well over 11 percent of the overall population, there are only about 3,845 black lawyers in the country comprising about 1¼ percent of the bar. See Christine and Leroy Clark, "The Black Lawyer," *Black Enterprise* (February 1973), p. 15.

erating major commentaries on black people and their legal situation ignore and pass over all black scholars, writers, and practitioners in the decision of who will structure, guide, and control the content and nature of that publication. The audacity involved is overwhelming.

The lesson from the exercise of so much white power—in the legal system and in the legal profession—is that black people, the black bar, and the black law schools must reassert their right of leadership and their right to maximize control over the decisions affecting the lives of the black community. They must fashion an independent thrust based on a black perspective and on black priorities. All who wish to join in and contribute to the effort should be welcomed, for it is only in the pooling of all available resources that any real hope of eradicating racism lies. This can be the first step in the forging of a new majority, which will avoid the pitfalls of operating in a manner that perpetuates the very evils sought for elimination.

Sic semper tyrannis.

METHODOLOGY IN BLACK STUDIES

Henry A. Bryant Jr.

For years the question of legitimacy in a particular discipline has been closely tied to the concept of methodology in that distinct discipline. This particular essay will examine the question of methodology as it relates to Black Studies. It will discuss certain basic methods as: (1) The Study and Intensity of the Degree of Africanism, (2) Interdisciplinary Studies, (3) Creation of an Hypothesis or Hypothetical Situations, and (4) The novel.

A new method which is yet to be tested will also be explained. It has been entitled, "Personal Observations of Collected Empirical Data," and is an entirely new approach conceived of by the author.

The question of methodology is not unique. G.P. Elton writes: "Historical method is more than a recognized and tested way of extracting from what the past has left the true facts and events of the past and so far as possible their meaning and interpretation.

It is the way of turning the evidence to account, and though there is nothing about it, it is nevertheless rigorous and not to be confused with the so-called common sense approach of the intelligent and untutored enthusiast."[1]

This stunning quote clearly illustrates the distinct nature of serious methodology and its importance to the pursuance of serious legitimate scholarship.

Research and Methodology have prepared the way for real advancement for human dignity and perseverence. It has been the blue print for relations between nations. DuBois writes: "Until the scholar has prepared the ground by intelligent and discriminating research, the labors of Philantropist and statesmen must continue to be to a large extent, barren and unfruitful."[2]

To emphasize how important methodology in history, politics, and economics has been in relationship to destroying a nation rather than serving the needs of humanity, we need only look at the colossal efforts of so called white historical scholars. These historians have undertaken through considerable effort to brand the Reconstruction Era, mainly the emancipation of blacks as a hideous mistake. Frank Burgess in his *Emancipation and the Constitution* insist that the emancipation of blacks was a virtual monster, and possibly the most serious mistake ever made by American whites. His basic hypothesis was Nordic Supremacy. He wrote:

> The claim that there is nothing in the color of the skin from the point of view of political ethics is sophism. A black skin means membership in a race of men which however in itself succeeded in subjecting passion to reason. To put such a race of men in possession of state government in a system of federal government is to trust them with the development of political and legal civilization upon the most important subjects of human life, and body. This is in communities with a large white population, is simply to establish barbarism in power over civilization.[3]

This method used by Burgess of misconstruing facts to suit his own personal opinions, or to justify the inhumane and immoral mistreatment that whites have reserved for blacks in America is common. Nothing has received as much mistreatment, supposition, and innuendo as the Reconstruction Period. Such established historians as U.B. Phillips, Hubert H. Bancroft, and Albert B. Hart among others, have used the same particular method. It merely involves the following: (1) inadequate and superficial research methods, (2) being totally silent on positive aspects concerning blacks, (3) greatly illuminating and magnifying incidents of non-positive nature where blacks are concerned, (4) nostalgia, (5) deliberate falsehood.

This method of history has been highly successful.

Community College Social Science Quarterly, Winter, 1975

So successful that it has shaped the feeling of a whole nation of people. This certainly illustrates the power of method in research. However, these historians certainly don't deserve their lofty pedestals in the archives of scholarly men, for as the noted Harvard trained historian, Arthur Schlesinger has to say, "For as historians, we well know that ours is not wholly a neutral or antiseptic enterprise. The ideal of history is the full and objective reconstruction of the past."[4] The object of the white historians was to subordinate and virtually re-inslave a whole race of people by the shaping and molding of white ideology towards blacks. Men like W.E.B. DuBois knew the early value of method in Black Studies. It was to (1) present as Schlesinger said, the objective truth about the past, (2) to lift black people to a position of pride in themselves by placing before them their true history and culture minus the deliberate distortions produced by whites.

Carter G. Woodson had been chafing for years at the misconceptions and falsities about blacks particularly in the American textbooks and now decided to throw his full weight of knowledge against it.[5]

This appears to be the monumental although not impossible task of black methodology to do exactly what DuBois and Woodson wanted to do. Certain particular disciplines and situations lend themselves to certain specific approaches. This brings us to the consideration of the first approach: **The Study and the Degree of the Intensity of Africanism.** "Ex Africa semper a liquid novi," out of Africa comes something always new, was a quote of the ancient Roman historian Pliny from 23 - 79 A.D.[6]

Africa has given the world countless gifts, to name all of these, would be fitting subject matter of a book. To discuss a few we could safely start with mathematics as developed to its mastery by the Egyptians. Physics, as emphasized by the construction of the vast pyramids, and medicine which has as its true father Imhotep, and not the Greek, Hippocrates.[7] Even arithmetic was known by the ancient Africans. In June of 1957, an abacus was found among the ruins of a 8,000 year old Johango civilization in the Belgian Congo.[9]

The Study and Degree of the Intensity of Africanism refers to the study to determine to what degree African custom, history, and culture, has determined and still exist, and to what degree it actually exists in white society. It is the study to determine which so-called western tradition is really African. An example of this is clearly indicated by certain words. The word "goober" or peanut comes directly from the west African "Nguba," "Baba" means father in Swahili and Japanese. "Babuska" is grandfather in Russian. Did the Russian influence the Swahili or vice-versa? Did the Japanese influence the African? Such questions as these take careful answers which can only be answered through close research designed specifically at determining how Africa has influenced the speech of those particular cultures. Which words in American society are actually African? "Ma Ma" is a good example. It is definitely an African word which has not changed to any degree, not even phonetically.

There is no end to the possiblity of this method in language. However, we need not limit the method to language. It can also be used to study how much Africa has influenced and to precisely what degree Africanism has influenced the Sciences. A valid example would be the vaccination, and the study of Astronomy which dates back to the Egyptians.[9] It can be used in determining how extensive African cooking still exist in white society. What particular cooking traits did the blacks bring to America with them? Which ones of these still survive today? The particular uses of this approach appear limitless.

The second method is the **Interdisciplinary Approach** which is of great value being that it integrates the main disciplines of history, politics, economics, anthropology, and sociology. Due to the complex nature of western society in general, and the even more complex nature of racism, it appears that a complex approach or method to determine the effect of either or both on blacks has great value. Black experience in history is closely tied with the black political experience which is also an historical experience. The black historical experience lends itself to economic plight in the black community. The study of black sociology transcends politics, history, and economics. One shortcoming of Black Studies Programs is that this method is not exploited more. Individual classes overlap because of the nature of the black experience makes it virtually impossible not to do so. Students many times receive minute segments of everything in their individual courses, which makes it more of a collective experience. An interdisciplinary approach would exploit each individual discipline by outstanding scholars in each program in close proximity to each other. Students would not have to attend many classes to get a full education in Black Studies. Departments with only limited Black Studies facilities could greatly benefit from such an offering. Departments with highly developed specialist and large programs, might benefit less from such a program.

The **Hypothetical Approach** is more in line with the so-called traditional scientific approach. The creation of the hypothetical situation or the development of an hypothesis lays the groundwork for the pattern of research. An example of an hypothesis which has considerable merit is "that Africa was the mother of all civilization." The black scholar could begin from the premise that Africa was indeed the mother of civilization period. His antithesis would include a close examination all counter arguments or dialectics. The problem could be attacked from an anthropological viewpoint using the works of Leake and other great scholars who have proven that Africa was indeed the mother of civilization. The point would be to develop on suitable thesis and arrive at the projected synthesis. This particular approach heightens initiative and individual imagination, and presents an outstanding opportunity for the development of new techniques. The creation of the hypothetical situation could be hypothesis set to drama. A situation such as the stating of an hypothesis concerning institutionalized racism could be put to drama and acted out using the hypothesis as the basic plot. The hypothetical method has unlimited opportunities for development.

The use of the novel as a teaching tool is not a new approach, however, it is one which should be discussed in relationship to Black Studies. One basic problem of black students who enter the Freshman year is that many of them, due to no fault of their own, lack basic skills for success. Many are more than "turned off" by the traditional textbook approach, and the lack of attention afforded them by less than adequate instructors who simply don't care. The traditional lecture discussion approach negates any conceivable effort to learn, because the material if interesting appears to be too difficult and unattractive. The novel can fill a void here. Practically every conceivable area of Black Studies has been covered, and with great interest by the novel. In sociology, such classics as the *Invisible Man*, by Ralph Ellison and the *Foxes of Harrow*, by Frank Yerby can more than suit the situation. Students become much more interested when they can read something in story form. In history there is an abundance of material. In some limited fashion Kyle Onstonts, *Drum, Mandingo, and Master of Falconhurst* are interesting reading and offer some outstanding factual information which more than holds the attention of the student. The *Learning Tree*, by Gordon Parks and *Black Boy*, by Richard Wright are classics with proven educational value and outstanding readability. Success by the use of these materials has been notable.

The last method which will be discussed has not yet proven itself, in that it must be subjected to empirical scrutiny. However, the author because of some limited experience in his own class has no doubt that this particular approach can and will benefit to a great degree the instruction of students on every educational level from primary school through college. It is entitled: "Personal Observation of Collected Empirical Material and Media." It represents the expansion of methodology to meet new needs and motivate a greater number of students. During the off season, the author usually spends a great deal of time in the South. This time is taken up in museums of history and just plain touring of historical sites. By doing so, a great deal of materials has been learned that couldn't possibly be learned from books or lectures. What if such material could physically be transferred to the classroom and used in seminars or discussion groups? Even on a limited scale, student interest soars. Retention and motivation are significantly heightened when the subject is able to objectively view the material discussed in class. The awe of actually viewing such relics as slave shackles, whips, such as the cat-o-nine lives, or the bull and Black snake whip ingratiate and stretch the curiosity of the student beyond belief. Much could be gained by field trips to black areas of significant history such as, Allensworth, California, which could fill this void. Students are also fascinated by people who have significantly made history. The lecturer that has expertise from years of study can't compare to the supposedly ignorant ninety-five year old black male or female who was there and never received a formal education. The ex-slave or the son of the ex-slave, the World War I black veteran who was there is much more effective than the expert could ever be.

The media approach is not all together new, but remains largely unexploited. At Leswing Press in San Rafael, we've just published a book put to cassette tapes called, *The Streets of Oakland*, by the author. It represents a break away from traditional textbook material of those who don't care for it, can listen to the same material on tape in the schools media center. It would do much to motivate the student who simply doesn't like the lecture - discussion technique. I could provide individual attention to a greater number of students that could be given individual attention by the teacher. The tapes approach is meeting with some success at all school levels. It could be a boom to Black Studies.

In conclusion, methodology is important in any discipline. The development of the particular approach to such discipline can determine to what degree the limits of such a discipline can be explored. This can't be truer than in relation to Black Studies.

Henry A. Bryant, Jr.

FOOTNOTES

1. G.R. Elton: The Practice of History, Thomas Y. Crowell Company, New York, P. 67
2. Earl E. Thorpe: Black Historians: A Critique, William Morrow and Company, Inc., New York, 1971. P. 22
3. Walter Wilson: The Selected Writings of W.E.B. DuBois, Mentor Books, New York, 1970. P. 188
4. Arthur Schlesinger: "Nationalism and History" in The Journal of Negro History, Volumn LIV, January, 1969. P. 19
5. J.A. Rodgers: World's Great Men of Color, 1270 5th Avenue, New York 29, N.Y. P. 668 Vol. 2
6. Ibid., P. 24
7. J.A. Rodgers: World's Great Men of Color, 1270 5th Avenue, New York 29, N.Y. P. 1
8. Rogers, op. cit. P. 9
9. Ibid., P. 9

THE ATTACK ON BLACK STUDIES

A Paper Presented To The Western
Regional Conference On Black American Affairs

Henry A. Bryant
2/27/76
Laney College

TABLE OF CONTENTS

	Page
Introduction	63
Objective of Paper	64
White History Writer Syndrome	67
Too Few Black Historians?	69
The Myth of A Non-History People	71
Blacks and Their Heritage -- A Recent Concern Only?	72
Black Refusal to be Academic?	74
Philosophical Myth -- A New Weapon?	75
Black Studies as an Action Agency	77
Other Aspects	77
Some Suggestions	78
Footnotes	80

THE ATTACK ON BLACK STUDIES

INTRODUCTION

The attack on Black education certainly is nothing new. From the beginning when it was illegal to teach Blacks to read, to the Plessey decision relegating us to markedly inferior cauldrons called "schools," the attack on Black education has been an unrelenting one.

In modern times the struggle has in no way dissipated, but it has merely changed its "modus operandi." By this we infer that it has become more subtle, more intense, with much more at stake.

Within the past few years we've witnessed the rise of many Black Studies Departments, institutions, and courses. The very nature of Black studies suggested that its conception would be far from wont or evolutionary. Circumstances dictated that it be virtually injected into the curriculum of higher education, high schools, and grade schools. It surely could not have been conceived through any other means.

Black students of the middle and late sixties demanded Black Studies programs. The intentions of these students were honorable ones. Denied any legitimate knowledge of themselves, fed a steady diet of "Washingtonism, Lincolnism, Jeffersonism, and apple pieism," Black students were simply "fed up." Accustomed to inferior schools, undertrained teachers, little or outmoded equipment, with insensitive school boards and administrations who merely perpetuated an already decadent and life-destroying system, Black students wanted a change now. The "power structure" had stalled for over one hundred years, yet education, in the literal sense of the word, was not forthcoming, neither would it be without a "substantial" push in the right direction.

So in haste with threats of Revolutionary violence, the "shell" of Black Studies was instituted. It was not the full grown product, but a mere infant conceived under unnatural circumstances. Scholarship as defined by the major traditional institutions was lacking, however, it was a beginning.

OBJECTIVE OF PAPER

The objective of this paper is to point out the danger, direction, methodology, and structure by which these attacks are coming. It will objectively attack those who attack Black education by taking them to task intellectually. Last but not least, it is our objective to voice some possible solutions to fighting these attacks and building stronger Black Studies Departments and programs.

In the past few years certain articles have been published attacking the establishment of Black Studies Departments. We will review two of these articles and attack the biased statements within them. Probably the biggest attack on Black educational institutions has been from the media, who have shown a particular irresponsible attitude especially towards Black Studies.

Chew, Peter, "Black History or Blaming the Sambo Image on Whites," National Observer, August 1969.

This article was chosen because it was in the author's conception the most blatantly biased and anti-Black. Mr. Chew was at this time a staff writer for the Observer. Nothing is said about his background other than the fact that he had gone to Viet Nam and written about the experiences of Black soldiers there. It appears with almost absolute certainty that Mr. Chew has no particular expertise in History, especially Black History. His article takes the following points:

(1) Many in Black History are subjects of mythology.

(2) The condemnation of outstanding Black scholars and the justification of White history writers of lesser merit.

(3) The false allegation that there are too few Black Historians trained in Black History.

(4) The allegation that a subjugated people cannot produce constructive history, and that Black History is only history in the mass.

(5) That Blacks were only recently concerned about their history.

Mr. Chew's tactic represents not a variable but a virtual syndrome by magazines and other media devices to subject Black History, and Black Studies period to virtual nothingness. This is done by allowing this very pertinent subject to be handled by intellectual neanderthals, or more appropriately, non-intellectual barbarians. With the number of competent scholars in the field, despite Peter Chew, these magazines have no knowledge or sympathy for the subject matter. This is apparent as blunder upon blunder is made in the article. He conspicuously attacks Crispus Attucks' part in history as mythological nonsense. He states that it was Attucks' mad behavior that might have sparked the whole thing.[1] Certainly this is not the first time that Whites have sought to blame the whole thing on the "nigger." One could not reasonably expect any saintliness from Adams in this respect who was trying to save his client at all cost.

Chew takes extreme liberties when he states "even the most respected Negro historians are included to support this myth." John Hope Franklin of the University of Chicago declared in *From Slavery to Freedom* that there was a fugitive slave, who with his bare hands, was willing to resist England to the point of giving his life.[2]

Although Franklin might certainly appear slightly paternalistic, however, this certainly is in no way an out and out myth. This same story is held to be true by many of the greatest historians in the United States past and present. Chew cites Adams' defense of his client in the trial as the only evidence to declare the Attucks incident as being mythological. He constantly states that this historian suggests this, or this historian says that. These are unfounded assertions. There is no name given to the historian who supposedly makes the assumption that Crispus Attucks was not even Black, Mulatto or any thing of that sort, but that he was a full-blooded Natick Indian. It is amazing what great lengths history writers will go through to condemn anything Black. Who is the historian who makes such an assumption? Upon what premise is this conjecture justified? This is in itself evidence of poor research and scholarship. It appears that the only possible motive here is to elicit antagonism towards Crispus Attucks. Would the assertion have been any less mythological if he had been an Indian?

Benjamin Brawley in his classic A Social History of The American Negro, 1921, asserted the following about the Attucks situation.

> They could not forget that it was a Negro Crispus Attucks who had been a patriot leader in the Boston Massacre, or the scene where he and one of his companions, James Caldwell, lay in Faneuil Hall.[3]

Brawley was an exceptional historian, and one of the great pioneers of social history and social behaviorism. He was no passionate militant whose views were obscured by rhetorical gibberish. Eric Lincoln in the introduction writes of him:

> Brawley must still be considered partial in the way developing Black scholarship perceived Black Americans in relation to white America and the world. He was in no sense a flaming radical -- even for his times.[4]

If there was any mythology here, it is almost certain that a historian of Brawley's character would have caught it.

Furthermore, in Leslie Fishel's and Benjamin Quarles' The Black American A Documentary History, 1974, an eyewitness by the name of Andrew states that Attucks was a mulatto and that it was he who was shot first.[5] This testimony was given at the trial of the British soldiers. How could Mr. Chew possibly not view this evidence?

J.A. Rodgers paints this picture:

> There was a conflicting story of what happened then but a clash followed. The crowd arrived with sticks of firewood, shouted angrily at the sentry, who shouted for the guard. Then later, heralded by Captain Preston ordered them to disperse. Attucks seizing the soldier with his fist. A soldier fired and Attucks fell mortally wounded.

The crowd shouted angrily. Advancing his
soldiers, Preston gave the order to fire
and four others were killed.[6]

From this quote it clearly indicates that Attucks
was the first to be killed as pointed out by Rodgers,
probably the most documented and meticulous historian
of all time. This certainly was no myth; it was reality.

WHITE HISTORY WRITER SYNDROME

Concerning point number two where the author of
this article condemns and omits outstanding Black historians in favor of white history writers who have no
knowledge of Black history or particular "love" or feeling for it. On page seven of his article he writes that
historian Eric Goldman sees the writing of American history as having gone through a number of ethnic cycles
with the accent on the Afro-American as just one more
"swing of the pendulum." In Goldman's view, he writes
it was too much to expect cool, objective history from
"underprivileged" groups that had begun to achieve
equality. Nevertheless, he continues, it was disheartening to examine some of the material that has been
"dug up" and offered as legitimate documentation for
Black History.

Needless to say, Mr. Goldman has never written a
book on Black History. He is neither to be regarded
as even quotable under these special circumstances.
If one wants to pick white historians of some repute
on Black History there are a substantial number who
might be judged as competent. Let us consider Professors Jordan, Litwack and Stampp of Berkeley. What
of Professors Frank Tannenbaum and David Brion Davis?
These men are passable. It is not to say that they
are entirely non-prejudicial on all aspects of history
concerning Blacks. On the other hand these Professors
Graham and Goldman to whom Chew alludes have no reputations whatsoever worth mentioning concerning Black
History.

Besides this, he clearly castigates John Hope
Franklin as so-called "going along with the myth of
Attucks." (p. 5). He cites Martin Duberman, Eugene
Genovese, and digs up a quote of Genovese's concerning
the flagrantly flawed <u>Nat Turner</u> by William Styron.

Black and white historians have castigated Styron's notoriously biased concept of the revolt in Southhampton. Genovese obviously angered by Blacks' reaction to Styron had this to say:

> . . . It is clear that the Black intelligentsia face a serious crisis. Its political affinities lie with the Black power movement which increasingly demands conformity, mythmaking and fabrication.

To assess these quotes we must consider these things. From the time of the Freedmen's Bureau White history writers have done an exceptional amount of mythmaking, fabrication and indoctrination. It is interesting to note that Mr. Chew talks only of these fabrications, "conjectures" and mythmakers. He even quotes Samuel Eliot Morrison's and Henry Steele Commager's The Growth of the American Republic, probably one of the most biased, crudely anti-Black pieces ever written despite the Pulitzer Prize given for it. It is virtual garbage and has no place with outstanding writings on history.

There are no quotes from W.E.B. DuBois, nor from the father of Black History, Carter G. Woodson. He mentions Woodson, but does not quote him. He never mentions Carter G. Woodson's The Miseducation of the Negro, or The Negro in Our History, and only briefly alludes to one of the most important historians in the world, W.E.B. DuBois. DuBois wrote countless works the most notable being his The Suppression of the African Slave Trade, The Souls of Black Folks, and The Gift of Black Folk. What of J.A. Rodgers and his outstanding works of history renowned the world over? No, but the author of this article chooses to use the enemies of Black people to condemn Black Studies. This is not the exception but the rule for many of those who attempt to attack Black Studies.

On page 105 he makes a considerable mistake when he attempts to cite some "well researched studies" on Afro-American History, his "representative" list of excellent works on Afro-American History. He cites Kenneth M. Stampp's The Peculiar Institution, 1956, C. Van Woodward's The Strange Career of Jim Crow, 1955, Gilbert Osofsky's The Burden of Race, 1967, and Leon Litwack's North of Slavery, 1961, as well as books by Franklin and Woodson. Why choose to give full names of books written by whites and mention the names of certain Blacks as simply an afterthought? The historians who were mentioned with their books are all whites, Woodson and DuBois are Blacks. Although he earlier alluded to the works of Woodson and Franklin, his inference was different.

Mr. Stampp's book while notable makes a serious error in the beginning where he describes the "Negro" as being a white man with black skin, which is certainly not true even if no offense was intended here. The fact remains that whites, however well intentioned, cannot choose for Blacks what is objective, natural history.

On page 105, Chew cites Ullrich Bonnell Phillips' thesis on the Plantation legend and states that Phillips was seriously "over flawed" and hesitates in calling him a racist and mythmaker, which was what he really was. Even Eugene Genovese in the introduction to the last edition of Phillips' <u>American Negro Slavery</u>, cited him as being racist. However, on page 105 Mr. Chew chooses to do what he himself assails some historians of being guilty of, mainly "even handed" justice. He is poignant with his remarks concerning the shortcomings of Black militants and Black Historians. However, his terminology softens remarkably when he mentions the cases of Phillips and Commager. The correct terminology for these men is white "racist supremist" and mythmakers, which they really are. He has given strength to these people by being guilty of "unevenhanded" justice and "overflawed" himself.

TOO FEW BLACK HISTORIANS?

The allegation that there are too few historians sufficiently trained in Black History gives over to two basic fallacies. First of all the quote by August Meir in the first half of this article is taken out of context. Dr. Meir alludes to the fact that Blacks avoided Black History. This is true because it was subjected to the same racist roadblocks. Today people will tell you, don't become involved in Black Studies because there are no jobs available in it. Up to now, Black education has been traditionally job-oriented, in that Black parents have constantly reminded their children to "get a good education so that you can get a good job." This has been the premise of the "calvinist edict" that rules the working class of this country. This emphasis was on a good "white education," they certainly were not considering anything Black. The jobs were those working for a white man. Black ownership and entrepreneurship were discouraged. Thusly most Blacks have been reluctant to even consider a career in Black Studies, a few courses in Black History, and certainly a Ph.D. in the program.

Men of great courage such as Carter G. Woodson were willing to suffer the ostracizing effects of dispensing the history of Black people, and raising it to a level of top scholarship, through The Journal of Negro History. Needless to say, racism, Black apathy, and discouragement plagued its early issues, but again courage and unmatched brilliance prodded Woodson on as he wrote,

> When I arrived in Washington, D.C. and began my research, people laughed at me and especially at my hayseed clothes. When I in my poverty had the audacity to write a book on the Negro, the scholarly people in Washington laughed at it.

This traditionally suggests the struggle of many Blacks who had great interest and skill in the area to reject it as a career, whereas white scholars who took interest in it were protected by their color. They had safe jobs in universities. The pursuit of Black Studies by white scholars was an accepted norm. Many of their books contained errors and innuendos which white people would accept. This is not true of all of them, however. They also being white could have their material published. Outstanding Black historians such as J.A. Rodgers had to have their own works published. Only the most courageous and dedicated wanted to deal in any aspect with Black Studies. Even contemporary publishers substantially shy away from truthful, authentic, forthright Black publications that whites count as unacceptable.

The next significant point here is how could Blacks in northern schools even study Black History? To a large extent it was taught solely in Black schools in the South. As research was being done for this paper,

we could not remember one Black course in any of the
high schools, junior high schools, or elementary schools.
However, this did not mean that there were no scholars.
At the conception of Black Studies Departments, there
had been already and continue to be now many outstanding
Black scholars. Many of them, of course, are not recog-
nized by "white America," but that is par for the course.
Some of these men are Rayford Logan, John Hope Franklin,
Benjamin Quarles, Leslie Fishels, Sterling Stuckey,
Ben-Joachin, Chancellor Williams, Basil Davidson, and
a host of others in the southern schools and universities.

Until 1947, there were no Blacks in professional
baseball. Did this mean that there were none present
of sufficient expertise to play? The Kansas City Mon-
archs beat the best white teams in baseball, year after
year. Josh Gibson was the greatest home run hitter in
baseball history. He was recently inducted into the
Hall of Fame, but what of Gibson in his prime? He never
got a chance to play, but he was there.

Many years from now undoubtedly a monument will be
erected to these forgotten people, who were there but
never received a chance. How many whites knew anything
about Black History? Besides the few mentioned here,
very few knew anything about Black History. There were
very few trained white historians with knowledge of
Black History when the Black Studies Departments began.

THE MYTH OF A NON-HISTORY PEOPLE

Finally Mr. Chew insists that a subjugated people
cannot produce history, and that Black History was
basically history in the mass. He writes on page seven,
"A subjugated people reduced to and held in a condition
little better than domestic animals is not likely to
make much history. . ." It is his contention that
Blacks brought here in chains from Africa, were until
our freedom after the Civil War, prohibited from making history, except in the mass of course.

First of all, Blacks were substantially a part of
American History prior to the foundation of America
in 1607. When the Spanish Conquistadores came, men
like Estevanico came with them. Twenty-five[8] per cent
of the men who came with De Anza were Black. Jean
Baptiste Du Soble was the first non-native American
in Chicago. He was the founder of the city, and he

was Black.[9] Africans did not come here as slaves prior to 1620. The history of Blacks in the United States prior to chattel slavery is substantial, and needs no qualifications. Many of these were individuals with nothing here concerning mass history. The idea that a subjugated people cannot make history is a serious fallacy. There is just too much proof to the contrary. Phyllis Wheatley, a servant of the Wheatleys, is an outstanding example of "individual achievement." Prince Whipple, Oliver Cromwell, and Peter Salem were heroes in the Revolution. They made history in a manner no less or no more conspicuous than George Washington.

Nobody allows anybody else to make history. People make history regardless of the circumstances. Blacks fought in all the wars of America. They killed the Indians as Buffalo soldiers (Henry O'Flipper), became heroes in World War I (Henry Johnson), were great scientists (George Washington Carver), and inventors (Norbert Rilleux, Lewis Latimer and others). Also Blacks were great athletes like Joe Louis, Jack Johnson and Jesse Owens. Certainly no one allowed Quaco, Denmarck Vesey, Gabriel Prosser, Toussaint L'Ouverture, Nat Turner, Frederick Douglass to make history. People make history regardless of restraint. It has been such from the beginning of time and shall continue to be so.

BLACKS AND THEIR HERITAGE, A RECENT CONCERN ONLY?

The allegation that Blacks have only recently become intrigued by their own heritage is the most flagrant lie in Mr. Chew's whole article. Witness the Black Renaissance with such literate writers as Claude McKay, Anna Bontempts, Langston Hughes, and Richard Wright. Frank Yerby wrote the best-selling novel The Foxes of Harrow, depicting Black life with respect to white encroachment. This is saying nothing of Clotelle or the President's Daughter, written in the nineteenth century by William Wells Brown. This was the first Black novel ever written. What of the old schools most famous writer George Washington Williams of the nineteenth century? What of the early American writings of Gustavus Vasta written before the nineteenth century? Delilah Beasley wrote the history of Blacks in California in 1912. W.E.B. DuBois wrote what was considered the first book of standard merit for Blacks,

The Suppression of the African Slave Trade, in 1896.
The proof is outstanding that Blacks have always been
interested in their history.

PART II

The next and final essay to be reviewed is one by
Mr. Ernest Van Den Haag, who is adjunct professor of
Social Philosophy at New York University. This article
is originally taken from The Balancing Act. The article itself appeared in The National Review, p. 970,
August 30, 1974.

Mr. Van Den Haag begins with the typical arguments
concerning Black Studies: (1) That Black Studies were
first of all taught by unqualified persons; (2) That
Black students don't want to meet the academic standards
set down by the traditional institution; (3) He is
basically concerned with mythical white standards of
prestige for the university instead of education per se;
(4) The supposition that unless whites control the "norm"
of Black Studies it is meaningless because less rigid
standards are imposed on Black Studies programs; (5)
He becomes philosophically absurd only in relationship
to Black Studies; and (6) He points out the real reason for white fears of Black Studies, the belief that
Black Studies institutions lead to action which he
feels has no place in the university.

Mr. Van Den Haag's arguments concerning the conception of Black Studies are basically the same as
those of Mr. Chew. Mainly that Black Studies was a
"forced" concession and that it really had academically unqualified persons doing the teaching. The
term "unqualified" is an often quoted cliche by whites
where anything Black is concerned. This is not to say
that some departments did not have people that were
not as qualified academically speaking. If you use
the Ph.D. as a point of qualification, this is true.
However, a Ph.D. by no means implies excellence in
teaching. Even so, many departments have had highly
qualified persons from the beginning.

In the spring of 1968, when the first teaching
position came my way at San Jose State University,
a group of concerned Black students and faculty met
and set up a committee. Permission to begin a Black

Studies program had already been granted. This group planned a full degree program and the drive for outstanding faculty was launched. Not just any faculty, but the best available faculty. Certain committeemen toured the East and brought back outstanding individuals like Leonard Jeffries, Ph.D. out of New York University, who would eventually chair the department. Dr. Jeffries was a renowned scholar as was his wife Rosalyn, a noted artist, who landed a position in the Art Department. Charlene Young, author and present department chairwoman, came aboard with a Ph.D. Robert Allen, author of <u>Black Capitalist Awakening in America</u> and another Ph.D., also agreed to come aboard. The rest of the staff had at least an M.A. degree in their respective fields with traditional degrees in both major and minors. This was a Black Studies beginning and this certainly wasn't an unqualified group.

BLACK REFUSAL TO BE ACADEMIC?

The second area dealt with the alleged fear of Blacks to "risk" the same academic standards as whites. Blacks have successfully competed with whites academically since the time of John Russworm. It is absurd to believe that we could not successfully do so now. Van Den Haag writes:

> They wish as it were, to have a Black enclave in the white institution so that they could both pursue Black goals and be sheltered from the academic standards and demands, such as they prevail for non-Black students.[10]

We were Black students in white schools and certainly knew nothing of "soft grading policies." Having taught in Black Studies Departments for the past seven years, I know that such a statement is ludicrous as well as mythical. Black Studies programs on the whole due to tight scrutiny by the academic establishment has subjected its students to even higher academic standards than many white institutions. This again is a highly biased statement.

Clear examples exist as to the virtual plethora of non-academic white standards. In fact now the state legislature is considering degrading the units of many of these non-academic courses such as transcendental meditation, courses in the occult and others. In the fall of 1975, we had the displeasure to sit in on a so-called interdisciplinary studies course. The loose nature and unstructured application of the course was amazing. The students couldn't possibly learn anything, because nothing was being taught. The teacher appeared to be hanging somewhere between cloud nine and ten waiting on cloud fourteen, chanting what appeared to be a Buddhist hymn.

To buffet this one need only to look at the so-called non-traditional education structure. In many courses no academic structure exists, and students are graded on a highly questionable pass-fail basis which affords no evidence of being any more effective than the traditional classes. It goes right back to the "if they are under the auspices of the university name," then they are fine. Anything separate and non-white will always be suspect, despite any standards of excellence which might exist there.

PHILOSOPHICAL MYTH -- A NEW WEAPON?

Thirdly, Mr. Van Den Haag retreats to philosophical absurdity. He writes, "The University is a place committed exclusively to the process of analysis, and to reflection and not to action or commitment."[11] This is completely fraudulent. When was the university ever committed to analysis? It appears only where Blacks are concerned. The universities have consistently provided the leadership role in the study and production of scientific technology for war. Stanford University's budget has been filled with war-related research. Men like Shockley of Stanford, Herrnstein of Harvard, Jensen of U.C. Berkeley, and Eysenck of the University of London, are in no way committed to analysis in a way that suggests pure analysis. By the nature of their work they are most assuredly committed to anything but freedom for Black people and proving us "scientifically inferior."

In a show of criticism concerning the initial goals of New York University programs which stated that goals of Black Studies would be to develop outstanding Black students, Van Den Haag asked why are the outstanding students to be racially selected, and shouldn't the university teach students regardless of color? Why wasn't this question asked of the History Department or of the Mathematics Department? Philosophically, on paper, this is the question to ask. Mr. Van Den Haag knows, unless he was the first man on the moon instead of the astronauts, that education has never been applied to students regardless of color. It is absurd for him to ask this question of the Black Studies Department, when for decades before any Black Studies Department was advocated, white institutions and their departments were copiously guilty of "not" attempting to aid students regardless of color.

The author of this article becomes even more ridiculous when he suggests the following: "The most effective way to help Blacks and thereby the Black self-image is to foster not Black Studies, but "studies for Blacks." He suggests that Sir Arthur Lewis and Dr. Kenneth Clark both have recommended following this same direction. However, if this be true, it does not necessarily suggest that since these men have Black skins, that we should be any more awed by their shortcomings than any white man. This applies especially if such suggestions are totally unreal.

Let's examine such a premise. Black Studies suggests that the origin, nature, and direction of the course is Black. Studies for Blacks appear to have the same connotation as fountains for "coloreds" under the Jim Crow era. Studies for Blacks were typical studies. It included only what whites wanted us to learn. It had inferior, outdated textbooks, complete with many ill-prepared teachers, in one-room schools with no blackboards or other equipment. Yes assuredly they were studies for Blacks, because no white man would dare to touch them.

Secondly, what does Mr. Van Den Haag know about Black people improving their image? He is at "best" an impartial observer. There is no reference in this article regarding any personal experience with anything or anyone Black. There is nothing in this article that would suggest any personal experience of the author being a victim of racism of any kind. An image destroyed is a unique and personal thing.

BLACK STUDIES AS AN ACTION AGENCY

Last but not least, Mr. Van Den Haag shows the real reason behind this concern, and probably one which all white academicians have some fear of, and that is that Black Studies institutions and programs are an action agency. It appears that this fear of action only applies where Blacks or non-whites are concerned. One of the basic deficiencies of the academic establishment has been its inability to meet the needs of the community. Things wrong in the community demand action. If those educated in the universities and provided with the expertise to solve problems do not address themselves to these problems, then how will they be solved? Is the university merely to provide the wheels on which will travel the vehicles of corporate wealth? Is its purpose merely to provide the minds to put the parts together to run the corporate machines? This has been the real direction of the university, and not the analytical as discussed in this article. If Standard Oil needs twenty petroleum engineers, then the universities are geared up to provide that. Departments have been basically subsidized at the university in line with the priorities of corporate production. Nothing is more action-oriented than the R.O.T.C. program. These programs are not on campus to provide analysis, but to provide men to lead other men in war. He asks the question, "What about the Black Studies Institute as an action agency? The university can become an action agency only at the price of giving up its academic character."[12]

The world is fast changing. Now the needs have to be met. In reply to Mr. Van Den Haag, we say that if Black Studies Departments can provide the leadership to deal with poverty, racism, economics, poor health standards, quality education and others, then it should be action oriented. It appears that the traditional white studies have certainly not provided the action to deal effectively with these ongoing problems.

OTHER ASPECTS

Other aspects of the attack on Black Studies Departments have been through the dissolution or control of autonomy in the department. Five years ago, there were some 400 Black Studies Departments, today there are less than 200.[13] This has been brought about through denial of tenure to Blacks, and affirmative action programs that are not affirmative action at all, but which retard action. The device today more than ever appears to be the principle of dispersing Black Studies programs among all of the other disciplines. For instance Black History would be under and controlled by the History Department, with the teacher and course content selected by that department.

Articulation of courses from junior colleges many times will meet a roadblock. By this we mean that institutions refuse to accept Black courses which are not under the control of white traditional departments as reputable, viable courses. An example of this is at Laney College where over the years we have experienced some difficulty in articulating our courses with the College of Letters and Science.

SOME SUGGESTIONS

Meetings like the Western Regional meeting in Los Angeles is an excellent idea. Here members can plan strategy for the survival and upgrading of Black education. By this we mean that proposals and annual plans could be made for a joint thrust and direction, that all members and participants could follow.

A legal arm should also be established. Many of the problems regarding Black education are legal problems. An example of this would be to form associations which could hire attorneys to sue the University of California regents for their lack of affirmative action in respect to graduate education especially. The committees that sit in on dissertation discussions and admit Black students or don't admit them to graduate programs are totally white. It is a direct blast in the face of the so-called "progressive" Black population in the Bay Area to know that the University of California at Berkeley just issued its first Ph.D. in Political Science to a Black man. This is the year 1976. The time when whites could control Blacks in education is past. Not only should we push Black undergraduate education, but graduate education should be pushed for Blacks also. Many Blacks of highly competent nature are being denied higher degrees by the same type of racism that was used to deny Blacks entrance into undergraduate education. Last but not least we will end with this quote from the old Eldridge Cleaver.

> Our struggle to gain Black Studies Departments on college campuses, our struggle to have Black Studies added to the curriculum across the nation is a struggle that the enemy sees as a grave danger.[14]

THE ATTACK ON BLACK STUDIES

FOOTNOTES

1. Peter Chew, "Black History or Black Mythology," in American Heritage, Vol. 2, pp. 4-9, August 1969.

2. Ibid., p. 5.

3. Benjamin Brawley, A Social History of the American Negro, Collier Books, New York, 1921, p. 56.

4. Ibid., Introduction, p. 14.

5. Leslie A. Fishel, Jr. and Benjamin Quarles, The Black American, Third Edition, Scott Foresman and Co., Glenville, Illinois, p. 46.

6. J.A. Rodgers, Africa's Gift to America, Helga Rodgers, New York, 1961, p. 102.

7. _____, World's Great Men of Color, J.A. Rodgers, 1947, p. 668.

8. Jack D. Fortes, Afro Americans in the Far West, A Handbook for Educators, Macmillan and Company, 1971, p. 8.

9. Ibid.

10. Van Den Haag, p. 971.

11. Ibid., p. 973.

12. Ibid., p. 972.

13. Omari Musa lecture given at Laney College, December 15, 1975, Senate candidate from the Socialist Workers' Party.

14. Eldridge Cleaver, "Education and Revolution," in The Black Scholar, Vol. 1, No. 1, November 1969, p. 48.

THE I.Q. CONTROVERSY

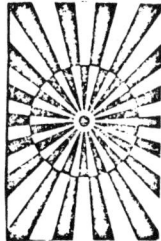

& SOCIAL SCIENCE

Henry Bryant

The I.Q. Controversy

The I.Q. controversy stated firmly carries the hypothesis that I.Q. (Intelligence Quotient) as measured by such tests as the Stanford-Binet Examination and the Wechsler Examination are largely due to genetic transmission through environmental influences. The argument further states that genetic differences are of increasing importance in the social stratification system of the advanced technological societies.[1]

The Genetic School

The main support for the genetic school (as the main supporters of the theory that genetics is the most important determinant for success in this society are called) is several studies of individuals with precisely the same genes, mainly identical twins born and raised in the same environment (MZ) and identical twins reared in different environments separated at birth by families with different social statuses.

There are the studies of fraternal twins (DZ) reared under the same circumstances as the ones previously mentioned. There are studies of individuals of no common genes, raised in the same environments. There are studies of siblings, fathers, aunts, and nieces in varying environments. The differences of I.Q. in these individuals appears to be roughly conformable to the genetic inheritance models suggested by the identical twins and unrelated to individual studies.[2]

The Environmental School

The second school is that of the environmentalist whose stance is that the present I.Q. examination structure denies the effect of the environment upon the I.Q. examination, which is basically regulated to white, middle-class standards. The environmentalists deny that the so-called mental gap between Blacks and whites (15 I.Q. points) is primarily genetic in origin, although is based upon an average variance. The basic premise is that the environmental considerations of cultural deprivation, racism, and denial of equal opportunity have a great deal to do with variances in average I.Q. scores between Blacks and whites.

Foundation of I.Q.

To better understand the I.Q. controversy, a close examination into its origin of one's intelligence maze is fully suggested and necessary to full comprehension within the scope of this paper.

The father of the I.Q. holocaust appears to be one Louis Binet. Binet seems to have tried everything that was available to measure individual differences. He was virtually obsessed with the phenomenon of difference. He once called upon a palmist to read the lines of the hands of approximately one hundred people. But out of this fiasco, through a shrewd process of trial and error, he sorted out those methods which best suited his purpose. He was commissioned by the ministry of public instruction in France to devise an examination for the expressed purpose of weeding out the "duds" from the more innately bright students.

He had previously experimented with an examination devised by Sir Arthur Galton, but later abandoned it because it failed to test the more important concepts dealing with learning and reasoning. He experimented with judgment, problem solving, and above all, the ability to understand words and written material. He compared mentally ill children to normal children in his laboratory located at Perry-Vaclouse.[3]

In 1908, he and Theophile Simon published his

famous examination. It was basically addressed to a certain age group starting from age three to seven-and-one-half. The following questions illustrate some of the content of the examination:

Age Three Years
1. Are you a boy or a girl?
2. Touch your eyes, your nose, and your mouth.

Age Four Years
1. Are you a boy or a girl?
2. Repeat three digits.

Age Six Years
1. Is this the morning or the afternoon?
2. What is a fork, a table, a chair, and a house?

From the content of these questions one can see that he was addressing himself to a very narrow group. Forks, spoons, tables, and other things are not necessarily utensils essential to the maintenance of every basic culture.

The Terman Era

It was not Binet, however, who was going to make this testing procedure a household word, but was one Louis Terman, professor of psychology at Stanford University, who was going to cause the fur to fly. Terman was obsessed about I.Q. he and an associate, Catherine Cox, actually attempted to compute the I.Q. of a group of people who never took an I.Q. test, even those who had been deceased for a substantial number of years. Through a series of complicated and highly scientifically questionable procedures, he concluded that the computed I.Q. of Napolean was 145, and that of Abraham Lincoln was 150. Goethe got a super genius rating of 210. DaVince's was 180, and Galileo's was 185.

It was Terman who shifted the Binet scale to suit himself. After the examinations had been given in many European (whites) nations, he found that there was considerable difficulty in computing the same things for the same age groups.[4]

He shifted 25 of Binet's items to a younger age group, leaving only about 19 items that were originally placed. In 1937, he and a Stanford associate, Maude Merrill, after ten years of research submitted another change. More tests and more items were submitted and these tests were tried on willing white subjects in the Stanford area whose former I.Q. had already been recorded. He then submitted the test to approximately 3,184 people from all over the United States. All were whites and all were native born. Their parents were also native born. This went along with Terman's first test in 1911, where all were white subjects and all were native born.

It was through these efforts that the Stanford-Binet Form L and Form M were formally put together. In 1960, he changed certain basic discriminatory items (sex discrimination) refining all these items into a single scale.[5]

From the former facts, certain basic concepts can be derived. First of all, the tested subjects in the early formation of the examination were white and native born, both in Binet's examination and Terman's. This would suggest the infusion of certain environmental factors not relevant to genetics. Secondly, the fact that the changes in the examination came as a result of earlier examinations with white subjects strengthen the argument for the environmentalist to protest against even the basic formation of such a test on the basis of cultural and racial bias.

What one gets from such an examination is an established white norm. As Professor Robert L. Williams, Director of Black Studies and Professor of Psychology at Washington University in St. Louis, states, "I.Q. and achievement tests are nothing but updated versions of the old signs down South that read 'For Whites Only.'" College admission policies (SAT) test, and Graduate Admission Examinations (GRE) are merely items for excluding Blacks.[6]

Dr. Williams, who earned a Ph.D. from Washington University, stated that he was an I.Q. failure. At 15, he earned an I.Q. score of 82, which is about three points above the "tracking system." His counselor suggested that he take brick laying as a trade which was quickly denounced by him as undesirable.[7] Many Blacks have experienced the same results, and have gone past them to great success.

Geneticism and I.Q.: The New Racist?

Who are these people who are so virtually insistent upon popularizing the I.Q. concept again? We say again because the first scientific racists were clearly shown to be nothing more than psuedo-scientists. The concept of "Social Darwinism" was once used as the measuring stick for the "Natural" class order of American society. Behaviorism was largely born as an effort to undue the harm done by these early scientific racists such as Herbert Spencer and Thorestein Veblen, the high priests of so-called "Natural Selection," won national acclaim for their popularization of natural and justifiable racism.

Arthur Jensen

Today's scientific racist, a scientist who maintains that he has the "good" of society at heart, is Professor Arthur Jensen, Professor of Psychology at the University of California, Berkeley. He has to be given the limelight in this instance. In an article published in 1969, by the *Harvard University Review* called "How Much Can We Boost I.Q. and Scholastic Achievement," which was supposed to be a response to the failure of the Head Start Program.[8] In this article, Jensen raised the hypothesis that low I.Q. scores might be due to genetic defects with environment having little to do with it. He and a number of his colleagues have established a hereditability factor of 0.80 for the genetic influence on intelligence and 0.20 factor for environmental influences. The meaning of this is that genetics (genes and chromosomes) account for 80 percent of one's intelligence, and that this factor can be accurately measured by such written examinations as the Stanford-Binet examination. Environment (achieved intelligence) accounts for only 20 percent of one's intelligence which can be computed on a written examination such as the one mentioned above. However, Jensen admits himself that this hereditability factor is largely an assumption. He writes in a footnote:

> I am grateful to the University geneticist, Dr. Jack Luster King, for making the calculations which are based on the assumption that the hereditability of I.Q. is 0.80, a value which is the average of all major studies of the hereditability of intelligence.[9]

Certain questions have to be asked here. First of all, does the hereditability factor of 0.80 merely purport to intelligence? What reaction of the individual genes produce intelligence? Could it be that the 0.80 factor of hereditability covers the entire spectrum of heredity-mainly one's facial resemblance to one's ancestors? Does it cover the fact that one might walk like one's father, have eyes like one's mother, and show the temperamental state of one's grandfather? The list of variances appears limitless. We can be sure that the entire concept of hereditability cannot be met in the factor of 0.80 for intelligence.

Jensen attempts to take the steam away from the realization of possible error by assuming that empirical scrutiny of all facts dealing with genetics is unnecessary. He states very clearly in his book:

> Determining the hereditability of the characteristic does not at all depend upon a knowledge of the biochemical or physiological basis or through the precise mechanism through which the characteristic is modified by the environment. Knowledge of these factors is of course important in its own right, but we do not need such knowledge to establish the genetic basis of the characteristic. Selective breeding was practiced for years before anything was known about genes and chromosomes, and the Science Quantative Genetics, upon which of the estimation of hereditability depends, has proven its value independent of advances in biochemical and physiological genetics.[10]

From this quote it would appear that Mr. Jensen didn't care very much for careful scientific inquiry into his purported theory of genetics. This appears to be a major weakness for the geneticist—a penchant for inconsistency in research. Princeton psychologist Leon J. Kamist has recently carefully scrutinized the twin studies on which Mr. Shockley and Mr. Jensen base their work, that some of his correlation efficients remained unchanged to the third decimal point which was a mathematical and statistical impossibility.[11]

Jensen also hypothesizes that the difference in population statistics plausibly have genetic basis and that the history of the Blacks has subjected them to breeding which is basically dysgenic. However, one basic question arises here because these population statistics relate to a basic homogeneous population. To use the data gained in this stydy as a norm for all others borders on intellectual barbarism.

The inconsistencies of Jensen constitute sufficient material for a book itself, and is entirely between the scope of this paper.

Herrnstein

The work of R. J. Herrnstein, professor at Harvard, has to be considered as a hand-in-hand friend of the work of Dr. Arthur Jensen. He completely supports the work of Dr. Jensen. He writes, "His experience was firsthand, dating from when he had written on the hereditability of intelligence and had been treated like a moral paria instead of the scholar that he is."[12]

Herrnstein is a supporter for the so-called productive power of I.Q. scores. In his article entitled, "I.Q." in the *Atlantic Magazine* of September, 1971, he states that the I.Q. scores of children are a direct prediction as to determining the amount of schooling, high status, occupations, and high income. The basis for a great deal of his information comes from a test given to 1,500 white children with an I.Q. of approximately 150 and trackings of them over a 30-year period.[13] Herrnstein became even more ridiculous when he included life expectancy within the range of his predictability.

A question arises as to why only white children are used. Like Jensen, and Mr. Binet before him, white children appear to be the norm. How can a set norm determined on white, fully-advantaged children be in anyway possible a measuring apparatus for other children? Can it measure the predictability of a poor white child with an I.Q. of 150 in Maine who comes from a disadvantaged family?

Herrnstein visualizes a caste system based essentially on I.Q. which has been named a Meritocracy. He states that the Meritocracy depends not only upon inherited intelligence but also upon inherited traits affecting intelligence, whether or not we know of their importance or have the tools to gauge them.[14]

This would appear to be the old Jensenian argument for shoddy inconsistency. What other inherited traits affect success? If these traits cannot be accurately measured, how can the results gained through such tests to measure success be even considered until accurate gauges can be found to determine the success ratio of these other children?

Herrnstein, like Jensen, appears to contradict many of his own genetic arguments. He writes:

> Regardless of whether the I.Q. differences of occupational classes are mainly genetic or mainly environmental, it is clear that children do not fully inherit either the superior or inferior performance of their parents.[15]

If this be true, then the science of hereditability is like the proverbial cloud shrouded in mystery. This would deny the infrastructure of the Jensenian based studies of parents and grandparents as factors in heredity.

William Shockley

William Shockley is a Professor of Engineering at Stanford University, and Nobel Prize winner for his part in the development of the transistor. He appears to be even more controversial than Mr. Jensen. Being an engineer and schooled in mathematics, Mr. Shockley's position on genetics is merely the rehash of Mr. Jensen and Mr. Herrnstein in that genetics and not environment are the basic questions in intelligence. He agrees to the standard heritability computation of 0.80 for inheritance and 0.20 for the environment. His position, however, appears weakened because of his lack of any training in the social sciences, and his absolute ignorance in the field of genetics.

Shockley, like Herrnstein, adds something new to the field, that of possible abortion for that element in the Black community which represents the "lowest possible genetic inheritance averages." He argues that without the refining quality of white blood, the situation is impossible. Those Blacks who have sufficient quantities of white blood in them could become part of the total community.

Shockley, like his predecessor, Paul Plenpoe, felt that this genetic impairment in Blacks heightened the crime rate in the area significantly. With the infusion of white blood (duffy factor) and abortion, he felt the problem could be eliminated to some degree.

An ardent foe of Dr. Shockley's is Dr. Francis Cress Welsing, founder of the Cress Welsing theory, and professor of psychiatry at Howard University. She writes, "Dr. Shockley thus proposes that this unfortunate state of affairs should be controlled and corrected by the nonprocreation of Blacks which can be achieved if Black people 'voluntarily submit to sterilization.'"[16]

H. J. Eysenck

H. J. Eysenck is a professor of psychology at the University of London. He fairly prescribes to the basic ideas as do Shockley, Jensen, and Herrnstein. He writes that it was a fairly universal conclusion that family environmental differences account for a much smaller proportion of intelligence than do heredity differences. Such a statement is not universally accepted, not at all. Many geneticists, such as Theodosius, feel that heritability is something more akin to studies in animals rather than in human beings.

Eysenck goes into the inheritance factors concerning motor skill, social maturity, personality type, or any other type. The basic concern of Dr. Eysenck is that he is a believer in the same basic heredity theories as Jensen, Shockley, and Herrnstein.

I.Q. and Social Science

It appears that the concepts of hereditary and quantitative geneticism are a serious threat to undermine the very substance of empirical behaviorism. The father of social science behaviorism, Dr. John B. Watson, stated in 1924 that environmental conditions could override hereditary conditions in determining any psychological test.[17] Watson once made the statement that he could take any child from birth and with the proper environmental stimulation, make him a doctor, lawyer, professor, or move him in any possible direction so desired. From a point of absolutism, such a statement might be questionable, but it bears the essential meat of the behavioral environmental argument.

Geneticism appears to undermine the whole concept of the effect of environmental condition upon any creature. Monkeys used in laboratories at Stanford University are being taught to categorize, to think, and to select to the extent that is readily measurable. It can be questionable whether these qualities are genetically derived or the fact that the environmental concepts in the environment greatly add to them. It is ardent that the particular things now being done by these primates were not evident under any type of empirical observation while in the African jungles.

Oppression and Racism

The genetic argument fails miserably when it won't even consider the effect of oppression, racism, and deprivation of opportunity on the mean concept of I.Q. The 0.80 heritability factor undermines the essentials of equalitarianism, which has been the major thrust of the sociologist since the 1930's.

The hypothetical argument that inborn genes and not environment have the greatest significance upon the intelligence of people destroys the behaviorist argument that Watson and other social scientists have strived to protect and perfect. If this be so, then the idea of a society based on equality is a myth. The total experiment into efforts to bring about equal treatment for all individuals, by providing equal opportunity through equal access to all the human things in this society are no longer valid. The whole idea of social mobility then would have to be closely in line with one's innate ability as proven through I.Q. tests. The meritocracy stated by Herrnstein would then take its "legitimate place" in the society and would be the essential criteria for preferred treatment.

The geneticist then clearly fails to deal with the causes of empirically observed behaviorial differences.[18] He shuttles over them as highly insignificant. Jensen usually states that the environmental factors of even related Blacks in Africa produced certain dysgenic impairments carried over to Blacks in the U.S.

Ashley Montague, famed writer and sociologist, states that such reasoning is highly invalid. Although environments of individuals could be substantially different, the cultures of mankind were basically the same; that of fruit gathering and hunting.[19] It was true for the African, the European, and all other continents.

Major efforts of the geneticist to destroy the basis of equal opportunity are underway. Since they state that the sociological hypothesis—that as people's environments improve, people improve in terms of education, wealth, culture, and adaptability is invalid. If that is the case, then all "costly" efforts along those lines should be eliminated.

Professor Putnam has stated that programs for minorities such as EOP grants and university quota systems to admit heretofore deprived minorities is ridiculous. The idea being that genetically impaired people, except those with a sufficient quantity of white blood, benefit more from specialized programs (vocational) than they do from academic education.

Return of Darwinism

It appears that thinking along these lines closely approximates that of the "Social Darwinist." With their idea of Natural Selection; the whole concept of Natural Selection being that those with great natural ability automatically achieve status and wealth. Those without it naturally fall to the bottom. Again there were no considerations of racial oppression here. Blacks were on the bottom because they were less fit along with the Indians, so the story went. Racism had nothing to do with it. If Blacks wanted to, they could pull themselves up by the bootstraps.

The geneticist appears to reinstate this argument, but he basically goes deeper than Darwinism. He goes to the point of conception itself. The geneticist also points out that Blacks (except mulattoes) are unable to pull themselves up because of their genes.

Shockley advocates sterilization of Black women who show less of the white blood factor. In Oakland, he has estimated this factor to be 22 percent who have enough white blood.

Conclusion

The argument of the geneticist that behaviorism should be studied in terms of genetic hereditability strikes at the very heart of the social scientist who states that factors in one's society, environment determine how well one does on an examination based on the norms of that society, or how one's social mobility is structured, or how one might be affected by adverse, harsh determinants of that society.

To the geneticist, the harshness of the society, racism by whites against Blacks, oppression of the poor by the rich, have nothing to do with one's place in society. All the evidence produced in history, sociology, anthropology, and political science is completely disregarded as minimal. The danger is eminent; these people have to be stopped!

1. Alan Gartner and Fran Riesman, I.Q.: The New Assault on Equality, Perinnial Library, Harper and Row, New York, London, San Francisco, p. 12.

2. Ibid., p. 13.

3. Evelyn Sharpe, The I.Q. Cult, Coward, McCann, Geoghegan: New York, 1972, p. 36.

4. Ibid.

5. Ibid., p. 47.

6. Robert L. Williams, "Scientific Racism and I.Q., The Silent Mugging of the Black Community," Vol. 7, No. 12 of Psychology Today, May, 1974, p. 34.

7. Ibid.

8. Robert Cancro, Intelligence, Genetic and Environmental Influences Greene, Stralton, New York, London, 1971, p. 267.

9. Arthur R. Jensen, Genetics and Education, Harper and Row Publishers, New York, San Francisco, p. 108.

10. Ibid., p. 118.

11. Stephen J. Gould, "Racist Argument and I.Q.," Race and I.Q. Oxford University Press, Oxford, New York, p. 148.

12. R. J. Herrnstein, I.Q. and Meritocracy, Atlantic Press, Little Brown Co., Boston, Toronto, p. 51.

13. Gould, op. cit., p. 87.

14. Cancro, op. cit., p. 22.

15. Herrnstein, op. cit., p. 53.

16. Francis Welsing, "Speaking Out on Black Genetic Inferiority," Sepia Magazine, May, 1974.

17. Ashley Montague, I.Q. and Race, p. 34.

18. Ibid.

19. Ibid.

SCIENTIFIC RACISM, ITS DANGER TO SOCIAL SCIENCE

HENRY A. BRYANT

Introduction

The concept of scientific racism goes all the way back to Aristotle who suggested that black skin was a mark of cowardice and ignorance. It was manifestly applied in the 1500's by George Best and his theory of "Natural Infection" where he assumed that Black inferiority was not just an environmental concept, nor wholly dependent upon culture but a natural basic concept dependent upon blood, and innate faculties inherent within the Black man himself. This paper will deal with the efforts of the scientific method to prove there is an inherent difference in the mental and physical capacities of different races of people. It will also deal with the concept of scientific racism and its danger to the social sciences as an educational instrument for the lifting and service of mankind and the solutions as to what should be done about it.

Definition of Scientific Racism

Scientific Racism may be defined as a pseudo-science engaged in by Physical and Social Scientists through observation designed to prove the so-called inferiority of the dark races. This particular definition although not complete does primarily engross the limits and scope of this particular endeavor.

Scientific racism in modern times was originally conceived in Europe in the late 18th century flowered to some degree in the United States in an early period,[1] however, the South did not greatly acquiesce to it due to the fact that it was the opinion of the planters that the question of the "nigger's" inferiority was settled, he was inferior, so stated the planter.[2] It was not until after the Reconstruction period that the nation felt that it was now necessary to pursue the concept to a greater degree, and it wasn't until after 1900 that the United States of America's interest in scientific racism caught up and surpassed that of the European. This would have manifest itself much sooner had not the Europeans been primarily concerned with Eugenics and Evolution. The American racist fancied himself a true Christian, therefore, the "sinful pursuits" of Evolution and Eugenics was a blasphemous ungodly concept.[3]

The first concerted effort by an American concerning the concept of scientific racism was made by Dr. Josiah Knott, an Alabama physician and slavocrat who wrote the then heralded, *Types of Mankind* which was published in collaboration with the pseudo-Egyptologist Dr. George R. Gliddon. It was a stern effort to contribute to the antebellum South in the 1850's against the encroachment of the abolitionist. His basic hypothesis again was that the Black man was physically and mentally inferior to the caucasian, and antebellum scientists were in strict agreement with Knott's superficial and emotionally written treatise on Black inferiority. He had raised many an eyebrow with his theory that the Black man was not even a man, but that he was a separate species of man altogether. He was not a "homo-sapien," but "homo-Africanus" a distinct and separate species of mankind; an animal.[4] This hypothesis although unfounded and unproven to this day, would dominate and command a considerable amount of the attention of the pseudo-scientist in the 20th century.

During this early period between (1850-1870) the European racist continued to dominate the scene. In 1853, Arthur DeGobineau, a French Aristocrat and Count, published his landmark, *The Inequality of Races* which enjoyed wide popularity not only in Europe but in America also. Again, this was the period when the abolitionist movement was gaining tremendous strength on the American scene. DeGobineau attempted to establish a law for the rise and decline of civilizations. His thesis was that nation survived only as long as their blood line was pure and when this blood line was mixed this made a difference in that civilization. His chief disciple, Richard Stewart Chamberlain, used the same thesis in his *Foundations of the 19th Century 1899*.[5] Although this thesis would enjoy considerable success and great popularity in the 1850's, it would become a factor for great consideration in the United States until the 1890's and the early 20th century.

Another European which had a considerable effect upon American science in the early years of scientific racism was one Francis Galton, a Frenchman who wrote a book entitled *Hereditary Genius, An Inquiry Into Its Laws and Consequences*, he was to add his prognosis, to the then infant science of Genetics, applying the concept of race to it. A staunch follower of Charles Darwin, he asserted in this 1869 work that racial characteristics are governed by evolution, the same as laws of heredity. They tended to vary from race to race, he insisted, and the result was innate superiority in other races. Racial improvement can only come through genetically selective breeding. Blacks, he stated, were the most degenerate of all races of mankind. They were primitive, childish, stupid and impotent.[6]

Adolph Hitler would apply this same basic type of thinking in the 1930's and 40's, when he would call for genetic selection in breeding, as a step towards so-called racial purity. However, his major victims would be Jews, and not Blacks. Could it be that Hitler knew something? Mainly that the true Jews (Falashas) were black in color. It's amazing to note that Hitler applied and implemented the concept selective breeding with his "storm trooper," "Aryan Supremacy" concept in *Mein Kamf.*

The Beginning of the Darwinian Era

Probably no one had as great an effect upon the development of scientific racism than did Charles Darwin with his classic *The Origin of Species 1859*, it became the most often published and quoted authority for the scientific racist of all times. Some authorities have insisted that Darwin was not a racist, but a scientist only, however, such noted historians as J. A. Rogers insist otherwise.[7] The point was also hammered home by Simkins when he writes,

> Among the confirmers of the Doctrine of Negro inferiority were such distinguished Americans and Europeans as Thomas Carlyle, Joseph Arthur DeGobineau, Charles Darwin and Caesare Lombroso.[8]

Darwin's survival of the fittest concept was applied to all aspects of life. The business community incorporated it into their "dog eat dog," "laissez faire," "coveat emptor" concepts. Thorestein Veblen and Herbert Spencer, two well known American naturalists, applied this to their axiom of "Social Darwinism." Their hypothesis was that society like the animal world depicted the orderly relationship of man with the most fit to rule in those positions of power, and those less fit in the positions of non-power. This according to the Social Darwinist showed why Blacks and peoples of color were on the bottom because they were less fit to be on top. Things had an orderly means of finding themselves in the "Proper positions." Needless to say, they soothed the conscience and abetted the efforts of many a guilty racist. By 1900, Darwinism was the chief scientific authority of the scientific racism.

Capitulation to Racism

In the middle of the 1800's the "nigger question" or the question of the role of the Black man, began to gain increasing importance in the United States. It appeared that the scientist-racist would finally gain his long hoped for objective; complete white acquiescence on the question of Black inferiority. The South was willing to listen because of the sectional animosity produced by the outcome of the Civil War. The downfall had actually began with the "Compromise of 1876" when Rutherford B. Hayes capitulated to Southern political pressures with his betrayal of Black America. The Northern so-called liberals shifted their opinion to the right to keep pace with the South. They were drawn further and further away from Blacks in the names of political and economic expediency. The North was drawn towards the cause of sectional reconciliation with the South basically because Northern financial interest had been frustrated time and time again in its efforts to economically exploit the South. The "nigger question" was hindering this possibility by constantly producing sectional animosity between two factions. It had to be ended. The means to end this was to use the dogma, produced in abundance at this time, but the scientific racist, that the Black was inferior, lazy, stupid, shiftless, moody, dirty, and totally unprepared to adjust to the rigors of civilization. The vehicle by which this process of reconciliation would be accomplished was through the media. It was quite common in the 1880's and 1890's to find such well known sources as *The Nation, Harper's Weekly, The Northern Review,* and the *Atlantic Monthly,* sources which had previously shown some degree of concern for Blacks, now completely within the clutches of the scientific racist. The ideal of the lazy, stupid chicken stealing idiot, was drummed home repeatedly as they continued to bombard the white population. This undoubtedly greatly contributed to the reconciliation between the white North and the white South.[10]

This capitulation to racism was manifested in many different ways. First of all, it could be readily seen in the make-up of the courts. In 1875, the Supreme Court of the United States ruled that the poll tax was not an unconstitutional practice by the states. In 1883, the Anti-Ku Klux Klan was found to be unconstitutional by this same tribunal along with the Civil Rights Acts of 1875. In the words of the courts it was not their job to guarantee Civil Rights to Blacks. To them it was not a human or a federal question, but one which should be settled by the States jurisdiction. The real crime of the situation was that the high court completely diverted the true purpose of the 14th Amendment from the protection of Blacks to the protection of the corporations, between 1890 to 1910, only 19 of the 528 cases before the Supreme Court dealt with the actual rights of Black people while the rest dealt with the protection of privileged corporations. In 1894, the National Democratic Administration openly and blatantly destroyed the Reconstruction Acts of 1867.[12] Such cases as *Hall v. Decuir 1877*, and *Louisville, New Orleans and Texas Railroad v. Mississippi 1890* were added to the progress of the scientific racist, and an America suddenly gone beserk with racism. The crowning blow to the already badly battered Black came in 1896, when the Supreme Court in the *Plessy v. Ferguson* decision ruled that "Separate but Equal" was constitutional. It was not legally sanctioned that whites could legally grant separate facilities to Blacks as long as they were equal facilities which they never were.[13]

The Social Sciences and Scientific Racism

The physical sciences by themselves were unable to completely fill the needs. It involves the following: (1) Inadequate and superficial research methods; (2) Being totally silent on positive aspects concerning Black; (3) Greatly illuminating and magnifying incidents of nonpositive nature where Blacks are concerned; (4) Nostalgia; (5) Deliberate falsehood.

These historians were careless in research and highly uncritical in reasoning, but were highly successful, so successful that they shaped the opinion of a whole race of people against another race of people.

U. B. Phillips, one of the South's most "distinguished" historians, pushed the idea that Blacks were happy, submissive, light-hearted, amiable, ingratiating, and imitative. "The Negro's inborn temperament may have made his enslavement feasible" he wrote.[17] He described the Black man's life on the plantation as good and beneficial. He wrote: "The Southern plantation was a school constantly training and controlling pupils who were in the backward state of civilization."[18] Needless to say, this point represented the nostalgic point of view. It contained the old idea of returning to the "good old days." Phillips' assertion that the plantation was a school demonstrates the most perverted of many perverted historical views. Plantation life was a horror. The following quote makes this fact clear:

> Many masters tried first to demonstrate their own authority over the slave and then the superiority of all whites over Blacks. They continually told the slave that he was unfit for freedom, that every slave who attempted to escape was captured and sold further South and that the Black man must conform to the white man's every wish. The penalties for nonconformity were severe, the lessons uniformly pointed to one idea; the slave was a thing to be used by the superior race.[19]

This quote adequately illustrates the true nature of life on the plantation. It was really a living hell. It was nothing close to a school, or even remotely related to a civilized institution.

This passion of the historical racist did not just extend to the Southern historian. Hubert Howe Bancroft, a noted historian who was a New Englander with an abolitionist background, wrote an article in 1912, substantially attacking the Black man as an inferior being. He began by stating that the Black man in America was condemned a position of perpetual servitude despite any attempt by him to arrest himself from such a position. He writes: "However lofty his ideals, or high his aspirations he must wear the badge of ignorance of servitude, he and his children forever."[20]

Bancroft was guilty of the same basic things that Phillips was guilty of, mainly superficial emotional statements maintained by inadequate assumed rather than carefully researched facts. It was his contention that the slave was "rescued" by the slavemaster. He writes the following: "Slaves were obtained from the different tribes constantly at war with each other such as Mandinga, Congo, Senegal, and Nard."[21] First of all, "Mandinga" is Mandingo. The Congo, Senegal statements are deliberate falsehoods. The Congo is a place in South East Africa. Senegal is not a tribe but a place. Mr. Bancroft didn't even know what he was talking about. Even elementary research would have revealed this as an error. He was ignorant of African philosophy and history, yet was quoted often on this particular subject. When an African was taken into a family after being taken in battle, he could not be mistreated. He was considered to be a son. The African civilization was an extended family. A servant could rise to the head of the family, he could become a chief, or a nobleman. It was in complete reverse to the white system of "slavery." Bancroft also repeated the often theme of the "happy darky" when he wrote: "However horrid the crime of human slavery, however repulsive in all of its forms and unprofitable in its operations, the fact remains that the Negro was the chattel of the chivalrous South."[22]

Blasingame readily reputes and lays stones on this myth of the friendly master. The master adopted many plans to assure the submissiveness. He made the slave bow in his presence, and accept the beatings from his young white. He was whipped for disputing a white man's word, kicked for walking between two whites on a street and was not allowed to call neither his mother or his sister Mrs.[23]

This illustrates the real life on the plantation, for it was certainly not a place of happiness, but a place where Blacks were forced merely to exist, and not to live.

World History

Despite the influence of the national American Historical racist and the works of Bancroft, Burgess, and other historians, these men, no matter how good they were, did not reach the lofty pedestals of the two most outstanding historical racists, Latrop Stoddard and Madison Grant. To expedite time, we will deal with the exploits of Stoddard, being that he was the most well known of the two. Stoddard, BA, 1905, Ph.D. 1914, wrote in the realm of world history and had a paralyzing effect upon all historical racism. Stoddard's thesis was that the world civilizations rose and fell dependent upon the purity of blood. This was a basic reinstatement of DeGobeneau's thesis, but in much more detail. He asserted that "mongrilization" was the real fear.

He wrote such well known classics as *The Rising Tide of Color Against White World Supremacy,*" 1920, and *The Revolt Against Civilization, The Menace of The Underway,* 1923. Civilization, he insisted had been saved by the continued appearance of the superior races who had replaced the older denegerate nonwhite races.[24]

To this thesis was added the concept of teutonism which ingratiated the writings of many social scientists in the 1890's and the turn of the century. Teutonism was the concept that only those of pure white blood could enjoy the blessings of civilization, Democracy, Christianity, and technology. Blacks, they insisted were unable to cope with the white "norm" that mirrored these concepts. Carl Penka added something else to the concept of teutonism, that of physical appearance. Teutonism, he insisted was always identical to blue eyes, blonde hair, and very white skin. These were the true fathers of civilization.[25] This concept of teutonic superiority continued to spread being that it fit to the tee the ideology of the innate inferiority of the non-white races.

The "evidence" against the Black man by the anthropologist and biologist in the 19th century was aided by voices and writings of the psychologists of the 20th century. These men applied intelligence tests to soldiers in World War II and deduced that Blacks were 10.37 in mental age as compared to whites who were said to be 13.08 in mental age.[26]

The psychologists were eager to enter the field of mental testing to prove the inferiority or superiority of races. The concept of the mental test was first of all developed in Europe, and introduced into this country in the 1890's. R. M. Bache used a test developed in Europe in an attempt to determine race differences. His particular test would measure sense perceptions of Indians, Whites, and Blacks. His endeavor was to measure the reaction of each race to special electric sensors placed on the skin to test the speed of reaction of each one concerned. The Whites reacted slower than the other races, this according to Bache indicated that they were superior, because they were more deliberate. Blacks were inferior because they reacted quicker, as did the Indians. It would be interesting to note what would have happened had the whites been first; then, Bache would have merely reversed his conclusion.[27]

In 1897, 500 white children were compared with 500 black children on a test which evaluated rote memorization. The blacks did better. One scientist insisted that this was due to their older age. However, the overall conclusion by Stetson and his group was that blacks were better at mechanical memory and that whites were better at abstract thinking.

However, the concept of mental age was the big Breakthrough. In the year 1905, Alfred Benet and Theodore Simon developed a test to determine degrees of intelligence. It was to measure degrees of feeblemindedness. Standards were set up for different age groups, and hereby the concept of M. A. or Mentage was born. To the detriment of Schockley and Jensen's, Benet and Simon stated that environment and educational opportunity would undeniably affect the achievement scored substantially.[28]

In 1912, one William Stern introduced the concept of I. Q. or Intelligence Quotient which could be obtained by comparing mental age to chronological age. The Binet Simon test would ask a group of questions to children which 75 percent of the children of his age could answer, the scores would be based on comparisons of these particular scores. There was a distinct disregard for comparison of the groups in terms of environment, educational background, income or otherwise.

In 1916, after the death of Binet, Lewis Terman and his associates fashioned the Stanford Binet scale, which is the basic I.Q. test used all over the nation.[29] The chief proponent of these modern day examinations are Mr. William Schockley. Supposedly the I. Q. tests are supposed to show the following things about blacks: (1) No resistance to suggestion. (2) Ability to remember through rote, but less of an ability to think abstractly like whites. (3) Ability to make rhymes better than whites. (4) Less motor control than whites. They are just a few of the axioms which these tests are supposed to show about Blacks. Mr. Schockley states that these tests are used for the good of mankind, in that they can be useful in structuring society in the "night way."[29]

In the beginning of this section on the psychological racist, were certain statistics on the tests used in service. In 1917, they used the basic Alpha Test, and the Nonverbal Beta Test. These tests have been a spawning ground for abuse by the scientific racist. In 1968, at a symposium on racism at San Jose State University, Mr. Schockley cited two statistical studies in support of his views. Scores, according to Shockley, from Army tests given to Black draftees in 1966, supposedly showed that Black intelligence had dropped six percentage points from a similar study in World War I.[30]

Shockley's point of view is that the lowering of the I. Q. among Blacks was due to the so-called heightening of the birth rates in the Black community. He advocated a program of Eugenics or an improvement of hereditary qualities in Blacks through controlled mating and reproduction in the Black ghetto in order to halt the trend towards lowered intelligences.[31] He also has asked for a substantial amount of money to carry on his proposed liberal abortion program for so-called "Ghetto Women."[32]

The concept of I. Q. has also been substantially abused by Shockley's contemporary and much publicized Arthur Jensen, a professor of Educational Psychology at the University of California, Berkeley Institute of Human Learning, stated that "as a group Negroes test 15 points behind the mean (white) or mid-point—for whites or Standard Measurement of I. Q.[33] Jensen also restated the old thesis, that Blacks lacked the ability to think abstractly. So-called "abstract thinking" was related to the idea of being able to deal with higher forms of thinking such as mathematics and calculus.

Shockley's position on Eugenics goes back to the Stoddard thesis that the only way to upgrade Blacks was through interbreeding was the basic portion taken by Stoddard and De Gobineau. It was also the position taken by Adolph Hitler. Things bring to mind the redundant nature of the scientific racist, to repeat his predecessors constantly almost to the point of boredom.

Shockley and Jensen further disavow any reference to the environmental factors that might have an effect upon the performance of children on intelligence tests. He cites that Genticity is 80% and Environment 20% concerning heredity factors for intelligence, by this he meant to say that environment had very little effect on intelligence and performance, but the overall genetic make-up of the individual was really responsible for his performance. This point was driven home by George Putnam who charged that social programs aiding Blacks should be abandoned in favor of programs more in line with Black capability. The social programs tend to be the target of the neo-scientific racist.

Scientific sociology extended even further than psychology. The sociologist became involved to a great degree. Nathaniel Southgate Shaler and his teacher and predecessor Louis Agassiz led the way. Agassiz put together his well known theory of "Natural Antipathy." Basically, he insisted that whites possessed a "Natural Antipathy" for Blacks. Hatred of a superior race, for an inferior race, he insisted, was a natural and very necessary thing. On the other hand, "inferior people have a natural love for a superior people." He divided this concept of Natural Antipathy into two basic categories, personal characteristics and life style. Personal characteristics of Blacks he insisted were things like Blacks were lazy, stupid, immoral, sexually beastily, and promiscuous. His life style according to Mr. Agassiz, was that he was filthy in that he wouldn't clean his house. He attempted to initiate whites, in that he wanted to be white. He drank excessively, was moody and argumentive, and couldn't transfer anything of value to successive generations. This according to Agassiz was an indication of innate biological inferiority of Blacks.

The Battle Against the Scientific Racist and Solutions for His Elimination

In my conclusion, I would like to propose solutions to the ending of the Scientific Racism Syndrome. Scientific Racism endangers the social sciences because: (1) It is based upon superficial and emotional research methods designed to prove an illusionary hypothesis. The examples of Ullrich Bonnell Phillips and Josiah Knotts are two classic examples. (2) It has basically been entered into by pseudo-scientists who lack in the basic knowledge of minority races, and won't even engage in basic research. Hubert Howe Bancroft is a classic example of this. (3) It is basically redundant, with substantial duplication and repetition. This can be emphasized by the overlapping of De Gobineau and Stoddard's overlapping consensus on history and Shockley, Grant, and Hitler's thesis on interbreeding and heredity. (4) Its basic objective is not the benefit of mankind, but the subjection and domination of one race of people by another. Scientific racism fairly depletes the true value of the Social Scientist, by placing the future of its particular disciplines in the hands of those who have only the objective of hatred and violence towards others. (5) It will substantially affect future generations being that the Social Sciences are frequented to a greater degree than any of the other disciplines. The work of great men of peace will be substantially curtailed by these activities.

Some Possible Solutions

I. There must be an increased publication of the awareness of the Scientific Racist. Men like Shockley always have audiences. Those who wish to destroy their influence must increase their publications.

II. A need to fight the Scientific Racist with methods as sophisticated as their own. Rampant emotionalism and ignorance are not the tools. The trained objective minds of social and physical scientists should turn a greater deal of their time and concern to fighting the problem.

III. Organizations—such as the one which met at U.C.L.A. on March 29, 1974, will have to spread every corner of the globe.

1. Idus A. Newby, Jim Crow's Defense, Louisiana State University Press, 1971, p. 8.

2. Francis Butler Simkins, A History of the South, Alfred A. Knoff Co., New York, 1947, p. 506.

3. Newby, op. cit., p. 8.

4. Ibid.

5. DeGobineau, The Inequality of Races, London, 1915, p. 31.

6. Francis Galton, Hereditary Genius, An Inquiry Into Its Laws and Consequences, New York, 1869.

7. J. A. Rogers, Nature Knows No Color Line, Helga M. Rogers, New York, 1952, p. 21.

8. Simkins, Loc. Cit., p. 505.

9. William Chace and Peter Collier C. VanWoodward. "Capitulation To Racism," in Justice Denied. The Black Man in America, Harcourt, Brace, and World, New York, San Francisco, 1970, p. 188.

10. Ibid.

11. Simkins, Op. Cit., p. 504.

12. Ibid.

13. C. Van Woodward, Op. Cit., p. 189.

14. Newby, Loc. Cit., p. 48.

15. Ibid.

16. Walter Wilson, The Selected Writings of W. E. B. Du Bois, Mentor Books, New York, 1970, p. 188.

17. Kenneth M. Stampp, The Peculiar Institution, Slavery In The Anti-Bellium South, a Vintage Book, 1955, pp. 8-9.

18. U. B. Phillips, American Negro Slavery, New York, 1918, pp. 464-465.

19. John W. Blasingame, The Slave Community, Plantation Life In The Ante-Bellum South, Oxford University Press, London, Toranto, 1972, p. 160.

20. Hubert Howe Bancroft, Retrospection, New York, Bancroft Company, 1912, p. 367.

21. Ibid.

22. Ibid.

23. Blasingame., Loc. Cit., p. 160.
24. Newby, Loc. Cit., p. 56.
25. Ibid.
26. Simkins, Loc. Cit., p. 505.
27. Young, Carelene, **The Black Experience**, Leswing Press, 1972, p. 105.
28. Ibid., p. 106.
29. Ibid.
30. See Information on p. 18.
31. See Chart One.
32. See Chart Three, Part 4.
33. See Chart Two, Part I.